Active Stock Investing for Beginners

A Comprehensive Guide to Stock Market Investing and Trading, Unlocking Financial Success in The Best Way Through Strategic Active Investing

By **Brian Scott Fitzgerald**

Published By **Fitzgerald Publishing Group**

Dedication

To my mother,

Your unwavering belief in me has been my anchor in the stormy seas of doubt.

You've gifted me the power of dreams and instilled the courage to transform them into reality.

Your willpower has been my guide, and your love is my strength.

My life and achievements are all a tribute to you and the confidence you've instilled in me.

How to Make Money Online: THE SERIES

I created a series of 12 (twelve) books on How to Make Money Online.

Feel free to read any of my books in the series, which can be found on my Author page on Amazon

You can visit this link or Scan this QR code to get access

https://www.amazon.com/author/brianscottfitzgerald.

Contents

Your Free Gift.

Thank you for your purchase; I'm offering my readers the FREE PDF version of ChatGPT Prompts.

To get almost instant access, go to this website. https://go.fitzgeraldpublishing.com/opt-in-page-active

Or use your phone to take a picture of this QR code, and it will take you to the Website for your Gift.

Inside the book, you will discover:

- **3000 Prompts** To help you make even more money online.
- **Save time:** You can search for new topics to create content on ChatGPT.
- **Expand knowledge:** Our Package of ChatGPT Prompts covers various topics, from science and technology to art and culture.

If you want to make even more money online, grab this free PDF.

Wait, that's not all; just for buying this book and getting the free PDF above, you can also earn another free Book.

You can use your phone to take a picture of this QR code.

Use the latest AI techniques to uncover online innovation's future. Take advantage! "Beyond ChatGPT and 50 New AI Tools: The Ultimate Guide to Discovering Cutting-Edge AI Tools Beyond ChatGPT" offers endless possibilities. Explore a variety of cutting-edge AI solutions to transform your work. Discover advanced AI tools beyond ChatGPT on this thrilling voyage.

Grab this free book if you want to make even more money online.

Introduction

Congratulations on picking up this, my first of two Stock Market investing books. Thank you for supporting your time reviewing this material I've delicately, thoughtfully, and meticulously put together to help you resolve two significant problems. The first problem this book will solve for you is eliminating the information overload and a sense of overwhelm many new investors face. We've all been there. Way too much-contradicting information is being shoved down our throats at every turn. We want to invest, and we want some guidance to help make the process more transparent, but there is only a simplified solution now.

The second problem this book is designed to help you is to give you all the essentials you need, without the fluff and hype, so that you can build a strong investing foundation that enables you to start small and grow into your empire.

In the vibrant tapestry of our modern culture, where TV shows and films reign supreme, there exists an assumption that you already possess an intimate understanding of the intricate workings of the illustrious stock market. Discover the untapped potential of the stock market and unlock a world of financial prosperity. Navigating the stock market and its intricate workings can take time and effort for beginners. Gain a profound understanding of the market's inner mechanisms and unravel the enigma behind the rise and fall of stocks. Unlock the secrets of the stock market and arm yourself with essential knowledge before embarking on your investment journey.

Discover the captivating realm of the stock market, where a vast array of stocks eagerly awaits the discerning eye of the public. Immerse yourself in a world of limitless possibilities, where these coveted stocks can be effortlessly bought and sold across many prestigious exchanges.

Discover the art of astute investing - where making a suitable investment is the cornerstone of success. Elevate your financial prowess by embracing the power of a well-diversified portfolio. Unlock the potential to amplify your returns and watch your wealth flourish over time. Discover the art of investing, where the key lies in crafting a financially abundant future.

I once paid about $7500 to attend a weekend business mastermind here in the United States of America. On the first day of the mastermind, as we sat in eager anticipation, waiting for the organizing host and world-renowned business leader to start with some profound business concept, he placed a hammer and some nails in the middle of our round table. He said,

"Thank you for taking time out of your busy lives to spend a few days with me, discussing business secrets that will give you an edge over the competition. As we begin, I want to remind you that the best gift you can give your business is to understand, master, and deploy time-tested business principles. In front of you, there's a hammer and some nails. Don't look confused. This is the first big lesson of the day. Before you can ever construct anything of value as an architect, you need the vision in your mind of the type of building you wish to construct, and you need to know the fundamentals of building, complex geometry, design, etc. But you can't construct anything valuable if you don't know how to use basic tools like a hammer and nails, basic laws of setting up a sturdy foundation, etc. Once you know how to work with the basics, you and your team can set up a foundation that holds a bungalow, a mansion, or a skyscraper. The lesson for us as businesspeople is simple. Know the fundamentals first, clarify your vision, and implement those fundamentals. Then you can erect whatever kind of business you desire."

I recall being confused when he started that speech - Staring at the nails and hammer. I thought, "I paid thousands of dollars for a DIY lesson using hammers and nails?" But it made so much sense as I sat there and listened to him. I'm sharing this somewhat unusual and irrelevant story with you because I've seen newbies struggle to create long-term success over the last three decades or more that I've been an active investor. After all, they skipped over the foundations. It's more fun to jump right into the sexy aspects of investing or imagine how rich you will be. Still, I can assure you that learning the fundamentals enables you to grow portfolios that offer financial freedom. So, this book is going to talk about nails and hammers. The basics that you must grasp before any investment work can begin. It will show you the mindset you must have, the strategies you must develop, and the approach you must take with stock investing to save your hard-earned cash. This book is also meant to help you create a good understanding and relationship with money because you will only get very far if you have that. In simple terms, I've written the book I wish I had when I got into this game. You'll hear how I fumbled and failed repeatedly before figuring things out. The painstaking journey I've endured has been worthwhile because it's gotten me to this point and made me all the money I used to dream about, so I am incredibly grateful to be where I am. At the same time, I'm aware I took the slow boat to China. So, this book is a success if I can aid you along your journey, especially now at the beginning, so that you can avoid unnecessary pain and losses.

The big problem in our society is the fact that we want shortcuts. We look at big names like Warren Buffet and want to know the fastest way to get to where he is. And yes, you can learn what he did to help in your execution, but you will lose when you enter the stock market game with that approach. You'll find so-called gurus who dangle that golden carrot in front of you and promise they can get you to that level of success fast and help you avoid the learning curve. I encourage you to run in the opposite direction whenever you encounter such promises. Here's the truth: The learning curve is precisely what you need to become a successful investor. You don't want someone who shows you how to build a skyscraper or, worse still, helps you build a tower when you have no idea what you're doing. Why? Because as soon as you're done, it'll all come crashing down and bury you in it. The learning curve helps you understand what you're doing and why. You need different teachers along your path to help you on your journey of growth and success. Each will help you piece this puzzle together until you reach your ambitions. Given how noisy the world is today, how do you know where to begin or which material to consume and implement first?

Simple. Start by educating yourself and following principle-based guidelines that are time-tested and proven to work. Invest in a teacher, book, course material, or mentorship that you feel in your gut will empower and educate you enough so you can begin this journey with the most confidence and competence. That is my intention for you, and I hope this book helps you meet that end.

The Old World Versus the New World

There was a time when investing was considered a rich man's game. How to get rich isn't a class taught in school, yet it's what we all deserve to learn and experience. A few decades ago, when opportunities like investing were still traditional and inaccessible to people like you and me, amassing wealth was almost a fantasy. My parents and probably your parents were taught that you got a job and worked hard in one position until they retired. Maybe you can retire with enough money to last until you pass. Still, in today's world, thanks to technology and the internet, you and I can easily carve out a path of financial independence regardless of our current vocation, educational background, and even how much savings we have.

Whether you have lots of cash saved up already and a nice six-figure income or not, you can still start today and, in a few years, grow a very healthy portfolio. I know this is possible because that's how I began my journey. I don't come from a highly educated background, and when I made my first investment, I was more novice than many of the people who will read this book. I was smart enough to know I needed to educate myself, but I also knew it would take much effort because my ambitions were huge, and my resources were minimal. I pushed on, learned the craft, took it one step at a time, and more than a decade later, I am an active investor and trader. My investment portfolio in the stock market continues to grow. As you will learn throughout this book, stock investing can give you access to financial opportunities you never even knew possible. You can manifest the lifestyle you've always dreamed of if you choose the path and stick to it until you reap the rewards. Today I am not only buying and holding but also investing in ownership of privately owned businesses that I see real growth opportunities. I also have my toes dipped in some fascinating real estate deals. All these have enabled me to earn even while I sleep and retire from the typical rat race everyone struggles with. I travel overseas for half of the year and work from wherever I want. This used to be a dream that felt more like a fantasy for many years, and because I never gave up on myself, as I hope you won't too, I get to call it my "normal" life.

You Can Live Life and Build Wealth on Your Terms

By committing to the study and implementation of the knowledge contained in this book, you will finally have clarity on what it means to be an investor, what stock market investing is, and how to do it right. You'll have the necessary know-how and tools to help you adequately research and evaluate different stocks to make the right choices. By the end of this book, you'll have everything needed to start and succeed at being a stock investor to forge your path to financial freedom. If you're ready to create real wealth and eliminate confusion about what to do and where to get started, jump into the next chapter, and let's talk investing.

CHAPTER ONE

The Must-Know Language Of Investing

Let's talk about getting rich. When it comes to wealth creation, you have two main options unless you expect to inherit wealth. from a family member. Those two main options are: You either trade your time to make money in some way, shape, or form, or you find a way to have your money (little or large sums) make money for you. The school system only teaches us how to trade time for money. Through our direct involvement, tears, sweat, and blood, we can produce an income that mostly never leads to financial freedom and great wealth. Only a minority have been able to create financial independence following that first option.

The ideal scenario for us is to combine options one and two, especially at the beginning. And, of course, the holy grail we're all searching for is creating enough wealth and financial independence to fully step into option two - having money work for us. That's what billionaires like Mark Cuban and Warren

Buffet do, which leaves them time to travel where they want, work when they want, and truly live on their terms. Doesn't that feel great? I know it was one of my biggest desires as a young man growing up. I was sick and tired of seeing how troubled my single mom was.

I vowed to do everything possible to create a better situation for myself. At first, I followed the first option of getting a day job and trading my time for money. I quickly realized that wasn't going to give me the kind of financial freedom I craved, and slowly by slowly, I started to learn about wealth creation. I recall reading my first book on wealth creation, which introduced me to investing. I immediately got hooked, and I've been learning, growing, investing, trading, and creating my wealth ever since. I start this chapter with my story because I need you to realize that investing isn't an instant fix for your financial situation. This is about playing the long game. Investing will allow you to take the driver's seat and become financially independent. But only if you play the game right.

To play the game right, you must understand and align yourself with the game's rules. That's where we're going to start. There needs to be more clarity today, with more and more people talking about investing and trading with little to no proper understanding, and it often leads others astray. So, I know you already want to start learning how to pick and buy stocks, but I need you to exercise a little patience and appreciate the importance of what you're about to do here. And that is, give yourself a crash course on what stock investing means. Even if you think you know, read this entire chapter thoroughly because the first rule of making money as a stock investor is always to be ready and willing to learn. You'll lose if you're a "know it " in stock investing. You will win if you're a "learn it all" in stock investing. It is that simple.

What is Investing, and How Many Classes Are There?

Investing is very dynamic and evolving, so it's prudent that a newbie grasps the complete picture of investing before jumping into one. Although this book is focused on stock investing, there are various other ways you can invest, depending on your personality, goals, and risk tolerance.

To state it, investing is putting money to work for you. It is using your hard-earned money to purchase an asset, interest, or any mechanism that you believe will generate income and profit in the future. There are three types of investments that anyone can participate in, namely, Ownership, Lending, and Cash equivalents.

Ownership Investment

It's the one most people imply when they call themselves an investor. Ownership investments are the most volatile and profitable investment class; our book will focus on it—specifically, stock investment. Aside from owning stocks, you can also invest in starting and running a business. You can invest in precious objects such as gold or collectibles such as a signed LeBron James Jersey. If you buy these particular objects and collectibles intending to resell them for a profit, that is considered an ownership investment. The last example of an ownership type of investment is real estate, meaning apartments, houses, or other dwellings you buy to rent out or resell. Here comes an important distinction. Mortgaging a place to live in is not considered an ownership investment. It shouldn't be purchased with the expectation of profit, even if it will be appreciated with time. So, if you think your mortgage is an asset or investment, think again.

Lending Investment

It's a lower risk than ownership investments, that's for sure. However, the returns are usually less. As a leading investor, you essentially take on the bank's role. Examples of lending investments include bonds, which we'll discuss shortly, and savings accounts. Even if you only have a regular savings account, you're still considered an investor because you're essentially lending money to the bank. Of course, the return is relatively low, and you're probably not getting wealthy from this investment. Still, the risk factor is also close to zero because of the Federal Deposit Insurance Corporation (FDIC) that covers your back.

Cash Equivalents

These are highly liquid investments, meaning they easily convert back into cash. These types of investments are as good as having cash in your pocket. Examples include money market funds, which, although they have low returns (usually between 1% - 2%), also have low risk, and writing a check out of money market accounts is as simple as using your checking account.

As mentioned, you're here to learn the basics of stock market investing, which falls under ownership investment. But before we dive into everything you need to know about stocks, let's touch briefly on some of the previously mentioned examples, such as bonds, cash investments, and real estate, as well as other alternatives such as mutual funds, exchange-traded funds (EFTs), hedge funds, etc.

Bonds Investment

The simplest way to understand bond investing is to consider it a kind of I.O.U between lender and borrower. In this case, you, as an investor, will buy a bond, which is a fixed-income instrument that represents the load given to either a corporation or government agency, and they are obliged to pay you a fixed interest rate in exchange for using your capital. Bond prices are inversely correlated with interest rates, meaning when integrated rates rise, bond prices fall, and bond prices rise when they drop.

The borrower, also known as the bond issuer, usually provides a bond that includes the loan terms, interest payments that will be made, and the time at which the loaned funds, aka bond principal, must be paid back. This "time" is known as the maturity date.

All bonds have a maturity date determining when the principal amount must be paid back in full or risk default. Think of bond investing as a way for you to lend money to big organizations and the government. They usually use this instrument to borrow money to fund projects, build schools, etc. Bonds are among the top three common investment types. The other two are stocks and cash.

One of the great things about bond investing is that you can hold a bond only some of the way through to its maturity because, in most cases, you can sell it to other investors.

Cash Investment

If you are only interested in a temporary fix for your cash, meaning you need somewhere safe to keep your money for whatever reason, then this type of investment might be right for you. Cash investments are very low-level risk investments usually insured by Federal Deposit Insurance Corporation (FDIC). As an investor, you get a short-term (90 days or less) investment that is simple, easy to execute, and can provide a return in interest payments. Unfortunately, this return type is low compared to other investment types. I consider this one of the safest ways to preserve your capital. Certificates of deposit (CDs) and Money market accounts (MMA) are examples of cash investments.

Stock Investment

This book discusses what stock is and how the stock market works. But to give you a lay of the land, understand that stock investment is when you purchase shares of stocks (equity) in a company to benefit from a company's success. Think of it as owning a small piece of that company. Usually, the benefits come from an increase in the stock's price and through dividends. Only and always buy a stock that you feel fully convinced must increase in value with time. When you buy stocks, you are considered a stock investor and can be called a shareholder. If you do a good job choosing a stock that increases in value over time, you can sell the store for a profit.

Public companies sell their stock through the stock market exchange, e.g., New York Stock Exchange or Nasdaq. Investors buy and sell these shares among themselves through stockbrokers. Depending on the kind of stock you own, you may or may not have voting rights at a shareholders' meeting.

If you want to succeed as an investor, I encourage you to buy and hold for a long time. As the book unfolds, we'll learn how to make money in stock investing.

Mutual Funds

A mutual fund is a common type of investing that I encourage every young, ambitious person to consider doing. It's a relatively low-capital investment and can be a great segue to stocks and other high-risk investments. Investor.gov defines a mutual fund as a company that pools money from many investors and invests the money in securities such as stocks, bonds, and short-term debt. The combined holdings of the mutual fund are known as its portfolio. So, consider it as joining fellow investors to pool your money to purchase securities. When you invest, you get to own shares representing your part ownership in the fund, which determines your income. The good news is that you don't need much money to get started, and you still get to diversify because mutual funds allow you to purchase different kinds of securities with your capital. You also don't need to manage the investment yourself because there are professionals who care, allocate, and distribute the pooled investment into bonds, stocks, and other securities. With mutual funds, you can earn money through dividend payments, increased NAV, and capital gains distribution. One of the things I like about mutual fund shares is that they are redeemable. So, as an investor, you can always sell your shares back to the fund whenever you wish. They are also highly liquid so that you can convert a mutual fund into cash within a few days.

Exchange-Traded Funds

An exchange-traded fund, often called an EFT, is a collection of securities, such as stocks, that trade daily on the exchange market just as stores do. They are like a mutual fund, except they trade throughout the day and mirror stocks' buy-sell behavior, making them volatile. The value of an EFT can drastically change during a trading day. One of the things that makes an EFT special is that it can hold multiple underlying assets, which means you can quickly diversify because you can own hundreds or even thousands of stocks across various industries if you choose. Some investors prefer to focus on a particular industry or sector, while others prefer funds that offer different U.S. assets. Others still like to get funds that have a global outlook. Depending on whether you want to use your EFT to generate income, hedge, or partly offset risk in one of your portfolios, or for various other reasons, there's a suitable EFT that you can invest in. I find EFTs among the most popular type of investment because of the flexibility and ease of trading, not to mention the broad coverage they offer. An example of a famous EFT is the SPDR S&P 500 EFT (SPY), which tracks the S&P 500 Index.

Hedge Funds and Private Equity Funds

Hedge funds are special and considered by the market as alternative investments because they use different investment strategies to generate "alpha" (returns). They are usually set up as private investment limited partnerships open to a limited number of accredited investors. I don't encourage this for a beginner working with a small budget, as hedge funds require a significant initial minimum investment. The other thing is that your funds won't be liquid because, in most cases, you'd have to go through the lock-up period (meaning your money is inaccessible) often a year or more. Your withdrawal ability is also limited to certain specified intervals, such as quarterly or bi-annually.

On the other hand, private equity deals with funds and investors that directly invest in private companies or engage in buyouts of public companies, resulting in the delisting of public equity. A private equity fund consists of Limited Partners who typically own 99% of shares in a fund with limited liability and General Partners who own 1% of shares with total liability. Venture capitalists are a great example of this type of investment because they finance companies and start-ups through this form of private equity.

These are only a few conventional and alternative investments you can engage in to grow your wealth. As you've seen, some are easy to start, requiring little capital and offering low-risk, low returns. Others need lots of investment capital and high-risk tolerance. Regardless of your ambitions, I suggest you start slow and straightforward, even if you have more than enough capital to engage in activities such as venture capitalism. The reason is that learning the language, the rules of investing, and getting your hands dirty in a small way gives you priceless experience and insight that you can apply even as a VC. That's why I now encourage you to switch all your attention to stock investing. It's the best starting point any severe investor can have. So, let's start at the beginning.

What is a Stock?

Stocks, sometimes known as equities, provide shareholders with a stake in a publicly traded corporation. It's an interest in the company, and if you hold most of the shares, you have complete control over how the company functions. The stock market is a collection of stocks the public can buy and sell on various exchanges.

Where does stock originate? Public Companies issue stock to fund their operations. Investors that believe the company will succeed in the future purchase those stock issues. Dividends and share price appreciation are distributed to shareholders. They may also see their investment dwindle or vanish if the company runs out of funds.

A stock is a certificate issued by the appropriate governing body that states you own a piece of a company. When a company needs money, it has two main options for acquiring cash. It can borrow or raise money by selling some of its shares to interested investors. These shares are what we call "stocks" or equities.

When you buy a stock, you become the owner of shares in that company. It's an investment (a stock investment) that enables you to claim ownership. Stock is the name given to the valuable certificates issued by share capital companies to their shareholders to document their shares and partnerships. Stocks also represent a property or partnership. They are bought and sold on the stock exchange, although some can be privately acquired.

What Is the Stock Market?

The stock market is an aftermarket in which shareholders can sell their shares to investors looking to buy them. This is done on a stock exchange like the New York Stock Exchange or the Nasdaq. Traders used to go to a physical site — the exchange's floor — to deal in the past, but now almost all trading is done online.

When newscasters say, "The market was up today," they usually mean the performance of the S&P 500 or the Dow Jones Industrial Average. The S&P 500 index comprises 500 big publicly traded Companies in the United States, whereas the Dow includes the 30 largest corporations. These track the performance of stock collections and illustrate how they performed on that day of trading as well as over time.

However, while the Dow and the S&P 500 are referred to as "the market," they are stock indexes. These indexes represent some of the largest corporations in the United States, but they do not represent the entire market, which consists of thousands of publicly traded companies.

Investopedia defines the stock market as the collection of markets and exchanges where regular buying, selling, and issuing publicly held company shares occur. These financial activities are administered through institutionalized formal exchanges or over-the-counter (OTC) marketplaces operating under regulations. A more straightforward way to understand the stock market can be found if you consider that it's often used to refer to one of the major stock market indexes, such as the S&P 500 (an overall index because it represents so many blue-chip companies) or the Dow Jones Industrial Average (one of the oldest stock market index and also one of the smallest with only 30 companies). There's also the Nasdaq Composite index, which represents thousands of companies on the Nasdaq stock market. The Nasdaq composite is one of the most diverse indexes because it has more companies than the S&P 500 or Dow Jones. There's also Russel 2000, Financial Times Stock Exchange 100, etc.

You might read or see a headline on the news that says the stock market has closed for the day or has moved lower. Usually, this means that stock market indexes have moved up or that they've lost value. Because it's not easy to track every stock, these indexes include a section of the stock market, and their performance is viewed as a representative of the whole market. The up-and-down movement you'll hear about informs you whether the stocks increase or decrease in value in the marketplace. Of course, as investors, we buy and sell supplies expecting to profit through this up-and-down movement in stock prices.

How the stock market works

The stock market works similarly to an auction house in that buyers and sellers negotiate prices and make trades. It's really that simple. Where does this negotiation and business take place? We call it the marketplace. It's a network of exchanges regulated by government-approved organizations, and the most important ones here in the U.S. are the New York Stock Exchange and Nasdaq.

Approximately sixty stock exchanges are worldwide, but you'll probably only ever hear about the following five major ones. New York Stock Exchange (NYSE), London Stock Exchange (LSE), Tokyo Stock Exchange (TSE), Shanghai Stock Exchange (SSE), and Hong Kong Stock Exchange (HKEX).

Companies looking to raise funds will list shares of their stock on an exchange (a process called IPO which stands for initial public offering), and then investors like you and me get to buy those shares. Once we obtain the claims, we can sell these stocks amongst ourselves, playing the game of buying and selling, leading to a supply-demand scenario. The exchange tracks the supply and demand of each listed stock, which helps determine the price for each security. This is done through algorithms that take care of the price calculations or the levels at which stock market participants, i.e., traders and investors, can buy or sell.

As the buyer, you will offer what's known as a "bid," i.e., the highest amount you're willing to pay, which is usually lower than what the seller wants in exchange, aka the "ask." The difference created between your bid and the seller's ask is called the bid-ask spread. That's a critical term to remember, as you'll often hear it. For a trade to occur, you, as the buyer, must increase your price, or the seller must decrease the ask. Thus, the game starts between the Bulls and the Bears.

It would be best to remember that trading took place in a physical marketplace for a long time. That came with its own set of limitations and advantages. Nowadays, however, trading has gone electronic, and thanks to the advent of the Internet and online stockbrokers, stock trading has evolved and become more accessible. Each trade happens on a stock-by-stock basis, but overall, stock prices usually fluctuate because of news, political events, economic reports, and other factors.

CHAPTER TWO

Understanding the Type of Stocks and Stock Tables

Now that you know what a stock is and understand the stock market, let's thoroughly understand the different types of stores you can invest in. There are two types of supplies: common stock and preferred stock.

Common Stock

Common stock represents your funds and shares of ownership in the corporation you've invested in. As a joint stock owner, you are entitled to both the risk and rewards of ownership, but your liability is limited to the capital you contribute. With common stock, you have income rights meaning a residual claim on the company's earnings. You also have the right to elect the company's board of directors at a general meeting and vote on various corporate policies. In the event of liquidation of the company, you would be entitled to receive the remaining funds and assets of the company assuming all creditors, denture holders, and preferred stockholders have been paid. What you receive will be proportional to the number of shares you own. One last thing you should know about being a joint stock investor is that you will have pre-emptive rights. That implies you can purchase the company's stock before it becomes publicly available. I like to think of it as getting first dibs.

Preferred Stock

It is like the common stock with this crucial differentiator in many ways. And that is that with preferred stock, you would have no voting rights; however, you do get to claim more on the company's assets and income. So, when it comes to having a voice in the company or helping to shape its future, you have no say as a preferred stock investor. Some like to equate this investing to bond investing because, as an investor, you are usually guaranteed a fixed dividend in perpetuity. In some instances, you can even get repayment of capital in the event of bankruptcy or liquidation. But unlike bonds, this may or may not have a maturity period. The dividend yield of preferred stock is calculated as the dividend dollar amount divided by the stock price. It is often based on the par value before a preferred stock is offered. Usually, it will be calculated as a percentage of the current market price after it begins trading. If you're a preferred stock investor, you claim a company's assets and earnings more during liquidation. Also, regarding dividends, the preferred stock gets priority over common stock, and their tips are usually higher than those issued for common stock.

Another essential thing to know about preferred stock is that the issuer can redeem the shares from you after a predetermined price at a significant premium over the purchase price. You also can convert to a fixed number of common shares, something an everyday stock investor needs to be more capable of doing. So, while they are similar, subtle differences make them unique and valuable. Depending on your objectives, weigh the pros and cons before deciding which type of stock to invest in. Aside from knowing these two types of stock, you also need to understand what stores do.

What do stocks do?

As an investor, stocks are intended to make you a profit. Of course, you need to make the right choice and invest wisely. They are proof that you are in partnership with a company. The most critical rights stocks give you is the right to get a share of the profit. You get the best out of a company or business without participating in the bureaucracy, management, and administration involved in running a profitable business.

Understanding Stock Tickers and Stock Tables

To understand stock tickers, you must first know what a ticker is. I'm sure you've seen that scrolling text at the bottom of a business news show or those big electronic LED screens that display the rolling market in real-time, often used by traders to keep track of stock in movie scenes. And today, if you visit any financial website, it's likely that you will find the exact scrolling text with overwhelming information at the top of the site. Most people tune out these streaming data because they often appear confusing and never-ending. However, this data is crucial to us as investors, so you'll want to train your brain to process and understand that information. In essence, that piece of information is what's known as a ticker. A tick is created whenever there's a change in the price of the security in the marketplace, whether that movement is up or down. The stock ticker (which has its roots in the world of telegraphy and was patented and modified by Thomas Edison himself) automatically displays the ticks during the trading session. Given the enormous volume of foreign securities, what you'll often see, especially on television, are a few of the most prestigious companies and indexes. Before you get overwhelmed, here's a simple way of understanding and reading stock tickers.

For publicly traded companies, the ticker symbol with an abbreviation of the company's name will appear on the stock ticker instead of the company's full name. You'll notice that most ticker symbols are very close to the company name. For example, McDonald's ticker symbol is MCD.

Some companies, however, like to get creative with their

symbols since they can pick whatever symbol they desire. That's why the Cheesecake Factory's ticker symbol is CAKE, and Sealy Corporation (a mattress company) uses the symbol ZZ.

Another thing to note regarding ticker symbols is that different stock markets will have their own rules on how many letters the logo can have. For example, companies on the New York Stock Exchange have up to three characters, while on Nasdaq are allowed to have four or five characters. At some point, these different ticker symbol rules for each stock market posed a challenge that frustrated many investors. When a company moves from one stock market to another, e.g., from NYSE to Nasdaq, which is very common, it would be forced to change the ticker symbol to conform to the new rules. This created much confusion for investors, and so in 2007, the SEC (securities exchange commission) decided that companies could keep their ticker symbol if it had three characters. Any company with a one or two-character ticker symbol can keep the same sign even after moving to a different exchange.

Below is a mini list of leading companies you'll mostly see on the ticker symbol on any given day with their accompanying ticker symbol.

Apple - (AAPL)

Amazon - (AMZN)

Anthem - (ANTM)

American Airlines Group, Inc. - (AAL)

Google - (GOOG)

IBM - (IBM)

Walmart - (WMT)

JP Morgan Chase - (JPM)

Johnson & Johnson - (JNJ)

Intel Corp. - (INTC)

Visa - (V)

McDonald - (MCD)

Tesla, Inc. - (TSLA)

Facebook, Inc. - (FB)

What does the stock ticker data tell you?

Let's take an example of GOOG 12.4M 16655 ^ 12.50

GOOG - shows you the ticker symbol. These characters help us identify a company on the stock exchange. A three-letter sign means the stock trades on the NYSE. Four letters may indicate it traded on NASDAQ. In this case, our ticker tells us this is Google's parent company.

12.4M - shows you the volume of shares traded. It's how many stock shares are being sold that day. The volume amount is abbreviated as "K" (indicating a thousand), "M" (indicating a million), and "B" (indicating billion). This can change and fluctuate throughout the trading day.

1665 - this shows you the trade value. It refers to the price per share or the last bid price. Like the share volume, this can change rapidly and fluctuate throughout the trading day.

(^) - This shows the change in direction, indicating whether the stock is trading higher or lower than when the market closed the previous day.

12.50 - this shows you the change amount. It details how much the stock price has changed since the market closed the day before and includes both dollars and cents.

You might also see a percentage of the price change in some instances. Aside from the letters and numbers on the screen, you must pay attention to the color. Green indicates the stock is trading higher than when it closed the previous day. Red means it's trading lower than when the market closed the day before. White or blue indicates there was no change from the last day.

Stock Tables

Before considering yourself a real investor (yes, even before you can expect to make money), you need to know how to read stock tables. It's one of the first lessons you must immerse yourself in and practice over time until you become masterful. Stock tables give your insight into a particular stock's performance. When you know what you're doing, reading a stock table can help you spot opportunities and avoid losses. They can help you determine whether to invest in that stock or not. Depending on where you get your stock tables from, they might vary in the information and layout; however, there are certain critical pieces of information all stock tables must contain. Let's go over these.

Name and Ticker Symbol: This column tells you the company name. It's often written in total, and the stock ticker symbol will be present, which, as we said before, are often abbreviations of the company name or something that represents the company somehow.

52-Week High: This column tells you the highest price that stock has reached in the most recent fifty-two-week period.

52-Week Low: This column tells you the lowest price that stock has reached in the most recent fifty-two-week period.

52-Week Range: Within one column, it details the lowest and highest price the stock reached over the past fifty-two weeks.

Volume: This column indicates the number of shares traded that day. For example, if you see 1000, it means only 1000 shares were sold that day.

Average Volume: This amount will tell you about the average volume over a specified period (e.g., three months or a year) and is used to give you a more in-depth look into how the stock is trading.

Previous Close: This column shows the amount of the stock price traded at the last day's close.

Open: The stock price will be shown at the market's opening.

Day's Range: It will indicate price fluctuations of the stock on that day.

P/E: This column represents the ratio between the stock price and the company's earnings. P/E stands for price per earnings and usually gives us a strong indication of whether a stock holds good value. Pay close attention to this metric.

Day Last: This column shows you how trading ended for a particular stock on the day represented by the table.

Net Change: This column will help you understand how the stock price ended on that day compared with the trading price at the end of the previous trading day.

Dividend: This column shows you the amount you will receive in a tip per year, per share of stock. For example, if you see 1.00, you'll earn $1 per share of stock annually as an investor. The dividend may be paid out monthly, quarterly, yearly, etc.

Yield: This column shows the percentage of that dividend on the stock price. The result is important for income investors, and we calculate it by dividing the annual premium by the current stock price.

In some cases, you might find dividends and yield in the same column; in others, it may not appear. Whenever you don't see a dividend column, it indicates that the company doesn't offer dividends.

The High, Low, Open, And Close of Stock Charts

Stock charts are price charts that show you a particular stock's price plotted over a given timeframe. You can get your hands on daily, weekly, monthly, quarterly, and annual stock charts.

Day traders can access even more miniaturized charts, known as intraday charts, which can be as short as 5 minutes. But as an investor, you don't need to concern yourself too much with intraday or even daily charts because your focus is to spot long-term trends. Therefore, weekly and monthly stock charts are the best charts to start reading. Aside from learning to interpret the volume, stock symbol, and the specific exchange it trades on, you also want to get good at understanding the price movement. That's where price change comes into play. Regardless of the different flavors and styles of stock charts, each one will always display the price. The better you interpret this, the easier it will be to see the trendlines and make profitable investing decisions.

The price change includes four key data points: The high, low, open, and close, all from that day's trading activities. The "high" indicates the highest price, and the "low" means the lowest price during that session. "Open" indicates the price at the start of the day, and naturally, "close" shows you the price at the end of that trading day.

Stock Market Investing Terminology for Beginners

You must know the most used stock market terminology to become a great trader. Below are the main ones you want to start practicing and quizzing yourself on so they can become part of your daily vocabulary.

Arbitrage - The buying and selling of the same security in different markets and price points.

Annual Report - A report prepared by a company (intended to impress shareholders) that contains information about the company, including cash flow, management strategy, and financial situation.

Ask - The lowest price a seller will accept when selling a stock.

Bid - The money a trader will pay per share for a given stock.

Bear - An investor who believes a particular stock or the market will decline.

Bull - An investor who believes a particular stock or the market will rise. This is, of course, the opposite of a bear.

Bull Market - Trading jargon used when the stock market is in a prolonged period of increasing stock prices.

Bear Market - Trading jargon for the stock market being in a downward trend. Aka, the opposite of a bull market. When a stock price plummets, we say it's very bearish.

Beta - This is a measurement of the relationship between the price of a stock and the movement of the whole market.

Bid-Ask Spread - The difference between the bid and the ask of a given trade. It's that gap between what the buyer wants to spend and what the seller is willing to accept for a business.

Blue Chip - A company with a history of stable earnings, regular and increasing dividends, and an impeccable balance sheet.

Capital Gain - The profit obtained from selling any capital asset where the selling price exceeds the investment's purchase price.

Close - This is when the stock exchange closes to trading. For example, the NYSE and Nasdaq close at 4 pm Eastern, with after-hours trading continuing until 8 pm.

Dividend - A portion of a company's earnings paid to shareholders or individuals that own that company's stock. It is typically paid on a quarterly or annual basis.

An Exchange is where different investments are traded—for example, the New York Stock Exchange.

Index - A benchmark used as a reference marker for traders and portfolio managers. Examples include Standard & Poor's 500 and Dow Jones Industrial Average.

IPO - This is for Initial Public Offering, the first sale or offering of a stock by a company to the public.

Liquidity refers to how easily you can get into and out of a stock.

Market Capitalization - Commonly referred to as a market cap, it is what the market thinks a company's value is. You determine market cap by multiplying the current price per share with the number of shares outstanding.

Portfolio - A group of financial assets such as stocks, bonds, cash equivalents, commodities, currencies, and their fund counterparts (mutual funds, ETFs, etc.)

Quote - This is the latest trading price on a stock.

Stock Symbol - This symbol represents a publicly traded company on a stock exchange. It can be between one and four alphabetical characters: for example, Walmart.

Is WMT.

Volatility - This implies the price movement of a particular stock or the stock market. Highly volatile stocks have extreme daily up-and-down activities and wide intraday trading ranges.

Volume - This is the number of shares of stock traded during a particular time, typically measured in average daily trading volume.

Yield - Refers to the measure of the return on an investment received from a dividend payment. To calculate profit, divide the annual dividend amount by the price paid for the stock.

CHAPTER THREE

Why Should You Invest in Stocks?

We all enter the game of stock market investing for various reasons. Some of us are young and just starting in life, and we're intelligent (and ambitious) enough to realize financial freedom won't come from getting a salary with benefits. Others take a while to figure this out and get to the family planning (middle-aged) phase of their life, only to realize they need to do something if they want better retirement conditions. And, of course, some are already approaching retirement, and it's dawning on them that a new source of steady and increasing income is the only way they can enjoy the years to come. Investing in stocks is a great decision regardless of age, current income, or ambitions. And it all begins with a solid plan and your first dollar. The only way to grow wealth in modern times and achieve financial freedom is to either work hard and hope it will happen or take personal responsibility, learn to invest, and make your luck. As we said before, you can invest in many ways, but I strongly recommend investing in the stock market because of how well it has worked for others and me. The risks are higher than other investment forms, but the rewards and the return on your investment make it worthwhile. If you know what you're doing, stock market investing will help you achieve your financial goals.

One of the main things I enjoy about stock market investing compared to other types of investing, such as real estate, is how easy it is to buy shares of companies. All you need is a broker, a financial planner, or online, and they'll hook you up with an account, after which you're good to go. I also like the fact that you can sell your stock at any time. In trading jargon, we call it "liquidity." So, for example, if you need money fast, you can turn your shares into cash and, in most cases, with meager transaction costs. As the economy grows, your wealth will increase if you're an intelligent investor. And since investors buy low and sell high over prolonged periods, your ability to spot and invest in fast-growing companies that appreciate over time means you can amass wealth relatively fast. This is especially true if you invest in a company growing steadily and paying out healthy dividends. Of course, that's not to say there are no risks. Any investment carries certain risks, and it's up to you to determine how healthy your appetite is for risk-taking. With stock market investing, you could lose your entire investment. If that scares you and makes you sick, I recommend forgoing stock investing altogether and opting for something like bond investing. You also need to know that stock investing is a long-term game.

You can't expect quick wins and must keep your emotions in

check. Your ability to discipline yourself and keep your emotions out of decision-making is vital because stock prices rise and fall by the second on any trading day. Volatility and price fluctuations are states you must get used to. I usually encourage my clients to avoid continually looking at the price dips of stocks. In your plan, ensure you include a regular schedule for updating yourself on price fluctuations, but it is to a minimum.

Creating Income and Profit

For many who don't understand the game, making money as a stock investor is about picking the right stock, trading rapidly, and continuously obsessing about the indexes while glued to a screen. That's an excellent way to miss out on earning a lot of money. Why do I say this?

The industry benchmark for the stock market's average returns is 10%, which is impressive compared to other alternatives. However, that only applies to confident investors. Most people never make that much, and it isn't because the market is unfair. The reason is that most investors behave like day traders. They need to be more short-term oriented and stay invested long enough for their effort to pay off. So, what is the secret to creating income and profit? Benjamin Graham said it best. "The real money in investing will have to be made - as most of it has been in the past - not out of buying and selling but our owning and holding securities, receiving interest and dividends and benefiting from their long-term increase in value." In other words, your time in the market will determine your overall performance. If you keep moving in and out of the stock market, the chances of doing it at the worst possible time and messing with your annual return are high. The more time, the more opportunity you have for your investments to increase because many companies tend to increase their profits over time. That, in turn, leads to higher stock prices, which translates into higher returns for investors owning the stock. So again, increased income and profitability as a stock investor is very much a game of dividends and yield. If you're the kind of trader that likes to trade in and out of the market daily, weekly, or monthly, then kiss those dividends goodbye because you probably won't own the stock at critical points that would enable you to capture pay-outs. That's why it's essential to figure out what kind of investor you'll be, what you care about, and what financial goals matter to you.

Financial Goals

While it's essential to become a successful stock investor, I've found nothing makes that journey of amateur to mastery more bearable than knowing why you're doing it. Chasing after money for the sake of it never brought anyone fulfillment and happiness, and it never will. So, before you commit fully to this journey, do a self-check, and figure out your financial goals and why you need to attain them. What's driving you? What's your why? How much money do you equate with financial freedom? We are all different, and what might be little money for me could be some- one's financial dreams come true. Take the time to identify your financial goals and write those down clearly. Here's a remarkable statement to help you align with your goals.

I want to succeed in my stock investment activities and grow a healthy portfolio to accomplish my goals and become financially independent. My main income/profit goal in the next five years of my investment activities is to have an exact number and state why I want this amount.

Identifying your short-term, intermediate, and long-term goals is also essential. Long-term goals would be classified as anything that needs funding five or more years from now. Intermediate goals will be the financial goals that need funding for two to four years, and short-term goals are less than two years from now. I'll remind you again that stock investment is best suited for people with significant long-term goals, such as financial independence or paying for a long-term project, etc.

Make It Your Business

If there's one mistake I want you to avoid that so many of us have been guilty of (me included), it is the inability to treat investing as a serious business. Stock investment is a serious business; those who take this approach will always win. Suppose you want to avoid suffering unnecessary loss or missing out on getting paid high dividends. In that case, you'll have to avoid taking advice from friends, forums, articles, and gossip magazines and instead educate yourself about stock market investing and how to do it right. One of the shifts I made when I realized I wasn't an investor is I stopped actively trading. For a while, I bought and sold nothing. I cut out the time I spent in forums and chat rooms and instead took up courses and read books about various companies and why they were successful. Companies that I wanted to invest in, like Wal-Mart. For about six months, I was busy learning how to manage a business at my local college, and over that training, I saw investing in a whole new light. I started to understand the fundamentals of running any business, and today, I've implemented many of those lessons across the different companies I now run over a decade later. Some of the things you want to start understanding about taking this new "business" approach include:

You are creating a business plan for yourself with appropriate goals and objectives. Clearly outline the program you will execute. Make sure it's thorough and details what you will invest in. Will it be stocks only or stocks and bonds? Will you only buy stores that pay dividends or mix and match?

Identify the income and profit streams, how you intend to pay yourself and your broker, and any mentor or teacher you need. In other words, determine your expenses and ensure they align with your income projections.

You also need to develop the ability to shift from strategic thinking to tactical implementation. Strategic thinking is the ability to understand the different possible market "conditions" and how various tools can be better suited for specific seasons in the market. It's also essential to develop a sound tracking system to track all transactions and their profit and loss, identify trends, see what works and what doesn't, etc.

Stocks Versus Inflation

Inflation tracks the price of goods and services and shrinks the dollar's purchasing power. That means when inflation rises, you can purchase fewer goods with the same amount of money, and as input prices go up, revenue and profits go down. The result is economic stagnation as things slow down until stability returns. Inflation is bad for everyone, including investors, because we pay more for less. The good news is that when it comes to stock market investing, you can protect yourself and your investments because, in theory, a company's revenue and earnings should grow at the same rate as inflation. If you're holding cash equivalents or similar investments, you are more likely to experience the hard blows of inflation. Still, if you've invested in the right stocks, you should be able to hedge off inflation seasons.

CHAPTER FOUR

The Basics You Need to Know About the Stock Market

When it comes to the stock market, there are two fundamental terms you need to understand and differentiate. They are trading and investing. These two terms are not synonymous, and it will be wise to understand what each word means and which of the two you want to focus on. This book is written specifically for investors of stock, not traders. There's a huge difference. Some people are successful in trading; others are better at investing; even fewer people are successful and naturally gifted to be great at both. You must deploy enough self-awareness to know which is best for you. I assume you know that being a stock investor is the right choice. So, let me give you a brief overview of some vital stock market concepts, including the difference between trading and investing in stocks.

Important stock market concepts that every newbie should know. Trading versus investing in a stock. The most significant difference between these two activities is the duration of a position. As a trader, you're only focused on participating in the game for the shortest time possible. You're looking for quick returns, so things like dividends and yields may need to be more relevant. As an investor, you care a lot about dividends and work. Your investments are generally meant to last several years. Although both a trader and investor are putting their money in the game expecting to gain profit, a trader's expectation may be as short as a few seconds up to a few weeks.

Conversely, an investor is most likely expecting their return within a year, a few years, or even a few decades. But that doesn't mean you can't buy and sell an investment for a profit next week. Just know that if you do, that's considered a trade.

Only when you purchase a security to keep it for a long time to experience the company's growth would you be considered an investor. So again, there is much overlap between these two terms, but it comes down to intention and timetable. The other thing I need to break down for you is the difference between stock trading and investing to avoid confusion once you enter the game.

The main differences between these two concepts are the return on investment, the capital investment, the risks involved, and the psychology needed to excel in either one of these activities. With stock market trading, you buy and sell shares in a company or derivatives based on shares in a company, expecting a profit. It is one of the most popular investments, and you would earn money in one of these two ways:

Price movement - when there's more demand than supply in the shares of a company, the prices usually rise. Investors in shares try to take advantage of these situations.

Dividends - as an investor, you are, in fact, a partial owner of the company, so you get your cut of the company's earnings and profits depending on the type of shares you own and the terms and conditions around it.

The two main ways to trade are becoming a day trader or a swing trader. Both have advantages and disadvantages. They also have equally long learning curves, so don't fool yourself into thinking you can learn both simultaneously. As a stock market trader, you must develop "good timing" skills and quickly act whenever the right opportunity comes. This skill benefits you from short-term market price changes, enabling quick profits.

Stock market investing

As we said, this is about investing in creating wealth long-term. So, what you will need is the skill of increasing prosperity and wealth through growing the interest and dividends of the company whose stocks you keep. I define the long-term as anything beyond three years. As an investor, you don't have to worry so much about daily price fluctuations of the stock price or the volatility of the market- place on a day-to-day basis. This means you can control risk a bit more than a trader.

Capital Gains

Capital gains are the profit you earn as an investor when you sell an asset like stocks, bonds, etc. When an asset's selling price (investment or property) exceeds the buying price, the result is capital gain. Another way to look at this is by viewing it as the difference between cost price (also known as the base cost of the investment) and selling price. You get capital gain when the cost and selling prices are high. By contrast, when the cost price is high and the selling price is low, we call that capital loss.

A capital gain can be short-term (a year or less) or long-term (more than a year) and must be declared in the income tax. Short-term investments in collectibles are taxed as short-term capital gains at ordinary income tax rates, while long-term investments in collectibles are taxed at 28% fixed. If your investment results in capital loss, that loss may lower your taxes a bit, but in general, capital loss isn't eligible for tax benefits. Capital gains have tax consequences on your investment, meaning your tax will depend on your tax bracket, asset class, and how long you have the asset. To understand the topic of tax better, I recommend you invest time and resources in a good accountant so they can help you figure out how to play the always confusing game of taxes as an investor. As of the writing of this book, governments around the world are trying to define Crypto for tax purposes better and whether they are like stocks, commodities, or currencies.

Dividend

A dividend is the annual profit distribution from stock corporations to their shareholders. This means that the companies distribute part of their profits to the shareholders every year. This "profit distribution" typically happens once a year. Every year all publicly traded companies get to decide whether they will pay out dividends and how high they will be. If a bonus pay-out was made in the previous year, it could go up or down, and sometimes it could fall back to zero, in which case no dividends would be given to shareholders. The more successful a company is, the higher the chances of getting reliable yearly bonuses. The stock-issuing corporation usually decides the amount of the dividend to be paid out on the day of the general meeting. Then it is paid to the shareholders a day later. As an investor, this is the treat you should be looking forward to, and it's your job to do your research well enough so you can own shares of a company that offers reliable dividends each year. Not all companies pay dividends, so if you find bonus payments attractive, pick a stock with this additional offer.

In recent years where low growth and low-interest rates seem to be the typical environment, getting stock that pays dividends has become a more attractive solution because they form a vital part of the return, we get on a stock market investment in the long run. Why? Because, with dividends, we can invest more by buying more shares, especially if we reinvest your profits properly. As a rule of thumb, I teach all my students and clients to reinvest their dividends until their portfolio grows to a desirable size. And if you feel like you can't reinvest all your profits because you have other obligations, that's okay, too; take a small portion and reinvest that because something is better than nothing. With dividends, you can also absorb possible risks or even losses at low moments when the market is weak. Another great reason to invest in dividend stocks is that most dividend payments have distinct tax advantages. Speak to your accountant to understand precisely how you can benefit.

Risks in Stock Market Investing and How to Minimize the Risk

All investment types carry a certain level of risk, but I'm sure you've heard the horror stories of people who lost everything when their stock investments went sour. Occasional market recessions and the natural volatility of stocks do not help instill confidence back into aspiring investors. So, I know there's a lot to worry about, especially as a first-time investor, but I can assure you that everything worthwhile in life will always carry a fair share of risk. If you have no appetite for risk and your personality and emotions are not resilient enough to withstand threats, consider becoming an investor. Whenever you stand to make a profit, there's always a chance that things might go in the opposite direction. If you know you want to do this but want to mitigate or minimize loss as much as possible, the following paragraphs should help you increase your confidence.

Reducing risk when it comes to stock investing is about getting educated about the stock, understanding the market, and thoroughly knowing what you're getting into before entering any position. Then, it's a matter of common sense, the right plan, and patience. Before determining what stocks to invest in, I recommend evaluating your potential investment and analyzing these high-risk areas:

Inflation risk

Inflation risk, aka purchasing power risk, rises when the cash you have today gets you less than it did yesterday. A recession usually leads to high inflation, which negatively impacts investments.

How to minimize risk:

Stock investing helps you mitigate risk as an investor because companies tend to adjust prices to the inflation rate. Something else you can consider doing is investing in U.S. Treasury inflation-protected securities, as this will mitigate inflation risk.

Liquidity risk

Liquidity risk arises when you buy an investment, decide to sell it to prevent or minimize loss, but quickly realize no one wants to purchase it from you.

How to minimize this risk:

Diversification can help you minimize this risk to a good

enough extent. For example, index investing can be a good alternative, where risk is diversified over the various stocks held within the portfolio. Consider ETFs such as the SPDR S&P 500 ETF (SPY) and the Vanguard Total Stock Market ETF, which offer such benefits.

Market risk

Market risk arises when the market turns against or ignores your investment. It also happens when stock market bubbles and crashes occur, which are extreme examples of what could go wrong in the financial markets. Unfortunately, this kind of risk is out of your control and can't be resolved through diversification, as with liquidity risk.

How to minimize this risk:

My best advice is to hedge your investments by taking a counter or offsetting position in a related security. For example, if you have a portfolio of losing and moderately volatile stocks, you can purchase an inverse ETF to protect against a market decline. The inverse ETF is designed to perform the opposite of the index it tracks, so in other words, if S&P 500 index increases by 5%, the inverse S&P 500 ETF will simultaneously lose 5% of its value. By combining your portfolio with the inverse ETF, any losses on your portfolio will be offset by gains in the ETF.

So even though market risk affects the entire stock market, the extent to which the market feels the impact can be minimized. Dividend exchange-traded funds such as the iShares Dividend

(DVY) or the Vanguard High Dividend Yield EFT are also great options to help you reduce this risk.

Economic risk

Economic risk arises whenever the market goes bust for whatever reason. And we know the market can go wrong anytime, so you always want to invest cautiously.

How to minimize this risk:

The simplest way is to add bonds to your portfolio as early on in your investment journey as possible. The founder of Essex Financial Services, John Rafal, claims that a 60%-40% stock-bond mix will produce average annual gains equal to 75% stock portfolio with half the volatility, so that might be a good rule of thumb to apply for yourself. Increasing your position in good, stable companies can also be an excellent solution to riding out these downturns. And, if the problem is domestic, consider getting into foreign stocks, which are known to work when the U.S. market needs to perform better.

Beginner Strategies That Will Make You a Better Investor.

Getting started as a stock investor can bring much excitement as you think about how bright your financial future will be as you gain more control of your earning power. It can also be overwhelming and confusing because of all the new lingo and the never-ending information you're expected to learn. Then comes the challenge of executing everything you learn, where many newbies get stuck. How does one know which is the right strategy to implement? The simple answer is that you don't. There is no one-size-fits-all, and the only way you can figure out which plan to go for will be a combination of how well you know your personality, how well you understand each of the strategy options, and what your current finances allow you to do. Top that with some common sense, and you'll be ready. While I can't tell you with certainty which strategy to use, I can at least simplify the main processes we all tend to use so you can see if any resonate with you. If you pick one and realize it's wrong, don't punish yourself by sticking with it. Switching to a new strategy should be relatively easy if you do things right. One of the things I like about investing strategies is that they offer much flexibility. Of course, take your time to pick the right one from the get-go to avoid the trouble of having to redo the entire process. Regarding stock investing strategies, the main ones are value investing, growth investing, dollar-cost averaging, and momentum investing.

Growth Investing

Growth investing is often considered the yin strategy because it's the opposite of value investing, which you'll learn about shortly. With growth investing, you're investing in stocks based on the intrinsic value of a company and its potential to grow in the future. As a growth investor, you should focus on young companies demonstrating their potential for significant, above-average growth and performance. Before deciding on a company, you must ensure it indicates real signs of growth and substantial or rapid profit and business growth.

A growth investor is often looking for "the next big thing," not recklessly or based on mere speculation, but rather through intensive evaluation of a company's current health and future earning potential and how that will impact the stock. So how do you go about identifying a growth opportunity to invest in? Simple. Look at the company's recent history. Is it growing? Is the stock value increasing? The company must have a consistent trend of strong earnings and revenue, implying the capacity to deliver on your growth expectations.

One of the downsides of using this strategy as a newbie is that, more likely than not, your chosen company will not pay dividends and bonuses. The reason is that companies in growth mode need capital to sustain expansion, which leaves very little for bonus payments to shareholders.

Tools to help you become a growth investor.

Use these five parameters to evaluate the company you wish to invest in:

1. Make sure the company has demonstrated a history of above-average earnings.

2. Check if the company's forward earnings growth or anticipated earnings for the next quarter match your expectations.

3. Make sure they effectively control costs while simultaneously boosting revenue.

4. Determine how likely they are to double asset value within five years.

5. Determine the current style of oversight deployed by management.

It would be best to equip yourself with specific financial metrics to become an influential growth investor. These include understanding profit margin, earnings per share (EPS), and your return on equity (ROE).

Value Investing

If growth investing is the yin, value investing is the yang in the investing strategy world. The value investing strategy is about getting the best deal at a discount. It's when you buy stocks from companies that the marketplace has undervalued. When I say a stock is undervalued, I mean that an analysis of its financial statements indicates that the price the stock is trading at is lower than it should be. That's usually based on the company's intrinsic value. As a value investor, you're. Therefore, a bargain shopper seeks to take advantage of the irrationality you realize exists in the marketplace. Warren Buffet is considered the ultimate value investor and is known to dig into his research for years before he's ready to invest in a company. But once he's ready, he goes all in. Buffet once said, "The market is a popularity contest in the short term. In the long term, the market is a weighing machine." When he's evaluating a deal, the main concern is the true potential and stability of a company. Buffet doesn't just look at the underlying price tag assigned by the market to individual company stock shares. Instead, he studies the whole company.

You don't have to do painstaking research to find a good deal, though, or what Buffest calls "on-sale" stocks. Various mutual funds and value index companies already do the legwork and allow investors to purchase undervalued stocks. The most important thing to remember is that you must invest in the long run. Just like Warren Buffet, when you decide to buy a deal, it's got to be a long-term commitment; otherwise, it won't work. And you should also only value-invest in stocks from reliable companies, not "unknowns."

Tools to help you become a value investor.

The price-earnings ratio (P/E) is one of the primary tools used by value investors to identify undervalued or "cheap" stocks quickly. To get the P/E ratio, you must divide a stock's share price by its earnings per share (EPS). A lower P/E ratio indicates you're paying less per $1 of current earnings, which is precisely what you should be looking for.

Many experts, however, will tell you this calculation needs more to identify a good deal. So, what can you do to ensure you're not being lured into a contract by false numbers? Researchers and experts suggest we use quantitative approaches to detect distortions like combining formulaic value with momentum, quality, and profitability measures. Of course, this is stepping into the advanced stuff, so don't worry if that feels a bit out of your wheelhouse for now. Start with the basics, and as you continue to educate yourself and do a lot more market and company analysis, using these approaches will feel manageable.

Fusing Value and Growth as A Strategy

No rule prevents you from devising a fusion between growth and value investing in creating your yin and yang combination. Warren Buffet has successfully demonstrated that it can be done. Historically, value stocks are companies in cyclical industries, primarily made up of businesses producing goods and services on which people use their discretionary income. A good example is the airline industry. People will fly more when the business cycle is on an uptrend because they have more discretionary income and fly less when it swings downward because they have less discretionary income. So, you'll notice that value stocks perform well during economic recovery and prosperity but fall behind when a bull market is sustained for a prolonged period.

Growth stocks, on the other hand, tend to perform better when interest rates drop and a company's earnings take off. Typically, you'll find that the stocks of such a company will continue to rise even in the late stages of a long-term bull market, but when the economy slows down, these stocks will take a beating. So, when creating your fusion, having growth and value investing will allow you to enjoy higher returns while reducing a substantial amount of risk. By investing in both strategies, you should be able to generate optimal earnings during virtually any economic cycle. Fluctuations in returns will likely balance out in your favor over time. If this sounds like something you can handle, then master both strategies and get to work.

Momentum Investing

If you believe winners keep winning and losers keep losing, you have the right mindset to implement a momentum investing strategy. This strategy is about riding the wave and going with the flow of the trends. In most cases, investors that prefer this strategy tend to be technical analysts because doing this right requires a lot of data and pattern recognition. We'll talk more about technical analysis later.

In essence, this is a concept that defies conventional wisdom. Instead of the usual buy low and sell high philosophy, this strategy adopts a buy high and sell higher mentality. It's based on the notion that you can earn long-term profits by riding stock while on a good run and then selling them once they've had a long bad stretch. From everything I've researched and even after speaking to experts on this topic, I still can't give you a definite answer as to why it works. All I can tell you is that it works - sometimes. And when it doesn't take momentum, investors suffer significant losses if they don't short-sell properly. Momentum investing doesn't work in every market environment, and momentum stocks are subject to shard reversals that can leave investors badly bruised.

If you use this strategy, be prepared to put in much work because it will take time, energy, and skills to research which stocks have been on a good run and still need to. For this to be accurate, you need specific complex technical indicators that tell you when to buy and sell a security.

Tools to help you.

As a newbie, if you want to test out this strategy without putting in all that technical work, you can start in a general way by looking at the trends and riding the ones that are rising. When the market is doing well, ride the wave. When it drops, stay away.

You can also follow the MSCI USA Momentum Index or the SPDR Russell 1000 Momentum Focus because such ETFs can help you use a momentum investing strategy without selecting individual securities.

Dollar-Cost Averaging

This is one of my preferred strategies; you'll see why in a minute.

Dollar-cost averaging is an excellent alternative for investors who don't want to or cannot afford to invest in a lump sum. With dollar-cost averaging (DCA), you're making regular investments in the market over time. For example, instead of investing $10,000 in a single transaction, you could invest $1000 monthly over ten months. Stock prices may go up or down during those ten months, but you constantly invest the same amount, and in the end, you'll have bought more stock when the prices fell at any given month and fewer units if or when the rates were higher. It's a great strategy to help avoid the overwhelm of trying to get "timing" right when investing.

It is not mutually exclusive to the other strategies I explained, which means you can execute whatever system you choose. Let's use the $10,000 example again. With DCA, you can put $1000 in an investment account every month to help you discipline your investment habits, and you could even automate the entire process.

This strategy enables you to spread out your stock purchases. That way, you can buy at regular intervals and in roughly equal amounts, so it helps smoothen out your purchase price over time and ensures you're not dumping all your money in at a high point for prices. It can be mighty in a bear market where you can "buy the dips" or purchase stock at low points when most investors are too afraid to buy. But here's the thing. It would help if you were committed and logical about this. Your emotions must be checked because you'll often need to act when the market or a stock is down.

I consider this one of the wisest forms of investing. This strategy not only helps you build wealth over time, but it's also a good way of neutralizing short-term volatility. This is especially true for newbie investors or people who cannot make a significant investment. If you have a 401(K) plan, you're probably already doing this or can have the option to do it.

To help you become a good DCA investor.

First, you need to decide on the total amount to be invested. Next, you need to determine the window of time during which the investments will be made, and lastly, select how frequently you'll make purchases.

Once you've identified your strategy (figuring out what's most suited to your needs, personality, and desires), it's time to go forward and start practicing. As you grow in mastery and expand your portfolio, you might realize it's time to add a new strategy or combine some of the ones we discussed. Feel free to shake things up a bit when that happens.

What Is Dividend Investing

In the simplest form, this is when you invest in stocks that pay a dividend, as we mentioned earlier. Dividend investing is great for new investors looking to generate steady income or build wealth by reinvesting dividend payments. By using dividend investing as your approach, you would only look for companies that can pay you a bonus. In doing so, you create a steady stream of passive income generated by the predictable income from regular dividend payments and the capital appreciation that happens over time. Dividend investing is a safe way of investing without too much risk and with a guaranteed return. The best advice I can give you is to make sure you buy great companies and avoid getting caught in chasing big dividends.

How to find dividend companies

The easiest way to find good companies to invest in is by setting parameters based on risk tolerance and objectives. There are no rigid rules here, but I will offer a few pointers that can help. First, I want you to look for healthy companies that generate free cash from operating activities, preferably those in development, i.e., increasing revenues and profits. Make a long list of these on a spreadsheet to start with.

I encourage you to look at the historical dividends and assess the chances of them being repeated in the next few years. Consider sorting companies in descending dividend yield and gradually discard those issuers who need to be promising to maintain historical results soon.

Next, I want you to prioritize companies with a clearly defined dividend policy, meaning the company declares that they will pay a specific amount of a particular part of net profit to shareholders yearly.

The other thing I want you to do is to dig deeper by going beyond "historical records" because playing in the stock market means you value the future but look to the past to make educated choices on which way to go for the best returns. Therefore, even though historical data does help inform you, it's wise to research these companies even more. I advise selecting companies for your portfolio after publishing the results for their third quarter. You can easily extrapolate the annual impact of most companies on this basis and estimate the potential dividend for the past year. With the knowledge of the current price, you can then calculate the future expected dividend yield. I also want you to study the company's balance sheet, including debt, cash, other assets and liabilities, and the industry the business is in. Is the company at risk from competitors? Is there a strong demand for their products or services? All this research will enable you to avoid the pitfall of choosing the wrong company, even if the yield and historical records look appealing.

Metrics to Help You Evaluate Dividend Stok Before Investing.

The dividend yield is the annual dividend typically represented as a stock price percentage. For example, if a company pays $2 in annual dividends, and the stock is $50 per share, the dividend yield would be 4%. ($2 \div 50 = 1 \div 25 = 0.04 = 4\%$)

Look for companies with a higher yield, but even more critical; as I just mentioned, finding a company that can maintain the dividend payments yearly is even more critical.

Pay-out Ratio

The payout ratio is the dividend expressed as a percentage of a company's net income. Suppose a company earns $2 per share in net income and pays a $1 per share dividend, and then the pay-out ratio, in this case, is 50%.

Earnings Per Share

The earnings per share (EPS) metric helps you understand how stable a company is. As a rule of thumb, you want to focus on a company earning more than its dividends because that's the only way to be long-term sustainable. The best dividend stocks are companies that have shown the ability to regularly grow earnings per share over time because it means the company can continue to pay its dividend and potentially increase it.

Total Return

The total return is the overall performance of a stock. It combines dividends and gains or losses from a share price change. For example, if a stock rises by 10% this year and pays a 4% dividend yield, its total return is 14%, i.e. (10 + 4).

P/E Ratio

The price-to-earnings ratio is a metric to determine if a dividend stock is appropriately valued. It divides a company's share price into earnings per share.

Regarding taxes, most dividend stocks pay qualified dividends, which depend on your tax bracket. While most dividends qualify for lower rates, some are classified as ordinary dividends and are taxed at your marginal tax rate. We'll talk more about taxes and investing later in the book. I want us to move to penny stock investing, which is extremely popular today.

Penny Stock Investing

What is a penny stock? According to the SEC (Securities Exchange Commission), this is the name given to any security valued at $5 or less per share. But for the most part, it is associated with ordinary shares of small companies that trade at low prices per share - usually less than $1- allowing an investor to buy and hold thousands of claims for relatively little money. Most of these companies are relatively new, have small market capitalization, and still need to establish a track record as successful businesses, making them speculative and high-risk investments.

The best part about penny stock investing is that anyone can do it. And I mean anyone because they are so cheap and easy to invest in. They can potentially yield huge returns for you. However, they can also lose all your money. Most of the talk you might hear around penny stocks isn't penny stalk investing. Instead, it's penny stock trading. There's a fundamental difference here to note because, in terms of risk and reward, it does make a difference whether you only want to invest in them or actively trade penny stocks.

I have realized that penny stock investing is worth digging into if you want to build wealth around smaller, less liquid companies. In the same way, some entrepreneurs are not interested in owning large multimillion-dollar companies; some investors wish to have small wealth-creation opportunities. If that's you, then penny stocks might be right for you.

A key thing about making money with penny stocks that most people get wrong is the kind of stocks they buy. You want to ensure you're investing your money in the right companies.

Characteristics of penny stocks:

High risk- high reward - It makes sense. Speculate types of investments will always be risker than usual. The counterpart to a high-risk investment is the potential for high rewards within a relatively short period. And it can be a manageable risk if you're smart enough to start small.

Small-cap - meaning they are typically tied to small-capitalization markets, which tells us that most companies you'll come across will have a stock valuation of under $2 billion.

Large bid-ask spread - The difference between the asking and bid prices with penny stocks is usually big, so you need to learn how to navigate this. Where to find penny stocks: Save your time searching for penny stocks on the primary market exchanges like NYSE or Nasdaq because you can only see the best ones through OTCBB and the pink sheets. What are pink sheets? Aside from the fact that the name comes literally since it originated as printed information on pink paper, these are over-the-counter versions of big market exchanges. Each day, the National Quotation Bureau publishes a pink sheet with the bid and asks prices for penny stocks and other stocks not traded on the more extensive market exchanges. In today's digital world, brokers can access the Electronic Quotation Service to check bids and ask prices in real-time instead of relying on that traditional daily publication. That helps when it comes to faster decision-making. Look for ".PK" after the company's stock symbols to identify a penny stock. In case you're worried there won't be many companies trading in this manner, let me assure you that there are currently more than 10,000 companies available and growing. Some investors also refer to Pink Sheets as the over-the-counter (OTC) market group.

Where to buy penny stocks:

Many people looking to get started need help figuring out the best way to purchase penny stocks. I recommend going for an online rather than a live broker. In the next chapter, we're diving into the world of brokers, so more on that later. But I discourage live brokers with this type of investing because penny stocks are incredibly low priced, which means profitability is significantly reduced if you use an expensive live broker. I suggest you learn, study the craft, and get good at trading. This is one of those situations where investing and trading overlap. And the line between being an investor and a trader gets blurred because, for penny stocks to work, the long-term buy-and-hold mindset fundamental to good investing practices must be re-evaluated. Penny stock investing is one of the investment types that should be treated as a short-term investment. This is especially true if you want to increase your chances of making money. That means you need to have an interest in active trading. So, before you get too excited about penny stock investing, consider the time, energy, and resources needed to help you succeed because this will be all hands-on deck. If you're wondering whether penny stocks are worth your time, let me remind you that some individuals (Timothy Sykes and many others) have shared that they made millions in profit from penny stock investing and trading. So, some penny stocks might result in losses; others might sell with little profit, and others will do well. The most important thing with penny stocks is to have a strong strategy that plays out over months so that you gain at a macro level instead of getting caught up in single wins. It's about investing in penny stocks and trading them collectively to make a profit.

How to find penny stocks to invest in:

As with all other types of investment, market research is what you need. The more you know about the companies on the Pink Sheets, the better. Start your research by sector, then the market, then individual stock. That helps you better understand competition, performance, financials, and more.

CHAPTER FIVE

The Best Online Brokers To Use

If you're serious about making money long-term and building a healthy portfolio, immediately start thinking about which broker you'll work with. Unless you're looking to go into mutual funds or using things like cash deposits and bank savings to invest, opening a brokerage account and establishing a relationship with an excellent broker should be the first order of business. That's because, with your brokerage account, you can access stocks in the stock market. And as we know, that's where the money is. So, before diving deep into brokerage accounts and stockbrokers, let's define a broker.

Who is a Stockbroker?

This person's primary job is to buy and sell stocks and shares for people who want to invest money. A broker can be a Company or an individual and usually earns by charging a commission for the services rendered when acting as a Company. A good stockbroker must be licensed by the body regulating the stock in their state. There are two broad categories of brokers. Namely, discount brokers and full-service brokers.

Full-Service Brokers

They offer a range of services, which include market research, investment advice, and retirement planning, added to a full range of investment products. This often leads to higher commission charges for their services. Some full-service brokers can charge as high as $600 per trade. You must think, "Who in their right mind would pay that much?" The truth is that a full-service broker may not be the cheapest in the market, but they may be what you need to succeed in this industry. If you're the kind of investor who needs comfort and much handholding to feel secure, then this kind of broker might be the best alternative - assuming you can afford it. Some of the benefits you would get include:

- Tax Preparation Strategies
- Opportunities to Invest in Off-Market Products.
- Retirement Planning
- Ability to Handle Unique Trade Requests
- Access to Initial Public Offerings
- Access to Exclusive and Proprietary Research Tools

- Experience.

Read that last point again because it's essential. When you're coming into the game as a complete newbie with no financial or investing experience, it does help to have a reputable company guiding you through the whole process. The only caveat you should know is that profitability will be constricted because the fees associated with these types of brokers will tend to eat up your gains. So, there's no right or wrong here. Determine your needs, the types of investments you'll be making, and the budget you can afford to spend before deciding whether to go full-service or discount.

Discount Brokers

There are many excellent discount brokers. I have used discount brokers for over a decade and have always accepted the choice. For the average investor building their wealth from scratch, this is usually the wise choice because they are more affordable and allow you the flexibility to oversee the decision-making process. This is a good thing when you want to control all the trades, but it also has its downfalls because you won't get professional advice. So, if you make a good choice, you win; when you make a poor choice, you lose. These brokers offer us the DIY (do it yourself) experience, which is great because you get to learn the ropes and dig yourself out of the trenches. Some of the best-known and most reputable brokers I can recommend include TD Ameritrade, Fidelity Investments, Charles Schwab Corp., and E-Trade. However, you can always do more research to find your favorite.

How to Choose Between a Discount and a Full-Service Option:

There's a lot to consider before making this decision. The first step is to answer these questions:

1. Do you want to go into a long-term investment or day trading plan? If you're planning on investing short-term, then a discount broker is probably the best, but if you're doing long-term investment plans, it's wise to consider full-service brokers.

2. How knowledgeable are you about the market? If you're a complete amateur, it might be worth investing in full service because getting that coaching and extra knowledgeable support will help you understand the investment world faster than going in unthinkingly.

3. What do you want to get out of your investments? Why are you investing?

4. What kind of securities are you interested in?

Now that you've answered those questions, here are questions to ask the brokers you shortlist to see who your best choice would be. What are the costs and fees associated with doing business with you? You must ensure your budget constraints align with the broker you choose. So that means you need to understand all the possible costs (hidden & extra costs) that might arise once you open your account—things like account minimums, withdrawal fees, fee structures, etc.

What kind of customer service and customer support do you provide?

What trading platforms will you have access to?

What educational materials will they offer, if any?

Should You Go for The Cheapest?

This is a question I often get because every investor is looking to make the most profit, and sometimes it seems like a good idea to go as cheap as possible with your broker. I have learned through experience that this is a more complex yes or no answer. The broker you choose can help you make a lot of money or cause you to lose a lot. Although discount brokers are more popular because they always have more affordable rates, they may need to match your investing style and needs. You may want to invest more in paying higher broker fees until you get the hang of things, then you can switch to something more affordable. Again, this will be a choice made at an individual level. Even among discount brokers, some will be cheaper or charge no commissions at all, but you should still go for that. Discount brokers are primarily suited to intermediate and advanced investors. They only work well when you take the time to educate yourself, as you're doing through this book and other materials and tools. Going for discount brokers is okay once you know what you're doing.

If I am to give you a single answer as to whether to choose the cheapest, my response would be - don't base your decision on price alone.

Do your research, and I will share with you in this chapter what you need to keep in mind as you pick your broker, but most importantly, go for a broker that helps you make the most money overall. Instead of worrying about how cheap a broker is, consider the following:

Your investment style - Are you a buy-and-hold or actively trading investor? What kind of investment will you use most of the time? Although most brokers offer a similar menu of investment options, deciding beforehand what you care about is essential. If you're primarily going to focus on stocks, ETFs, and bonds, then you want to choose a broker that offers good value. Pay extra attention to the commissions associated with your preferred investment style.

Account fees - most brokers will charge account fees, but some have better deals than others. Typical prices include annual, inactivity, trading platform subscription, research, data fees, etc. Make sure you know how much this will cost you monthly and annually.

Account minimums - Some brokers offer no account minimum,

for example, Ally Invest, Merrill Edge, and TD Ameritrade. Others require a minimum initial investment of anything from $500 and up. Find out what your broker offers.

Investing Online

It can be nerve-racking to start investing online regardless of age or how much money you've saved. I want to ensure you feel less nervous and more confident about this decision. Putting your money into investments is the best way to build wealth and save for your retirement, at least here in the United States of America. Here's how to map this process out for yourself and avoid the anxiety most people get, which often leads to procrastination. First, you need to decide why you're doing this. What's the main driving ambition here? Is it for retirement? Do you want to be actively trading as an investor or build a strong portfolio over a long period? Once you know your big "Why" for becoming an investor, you can decide how much help you'll need during your first year or two. Do a self-assessment and determine your strengths and weakness to know the best decision to make when choosing Brokerage Companies. Give your money long-term goals and short-term goals. Set a reasonable deadline for each of these goals. Educate yourself and surround yourself with the right professional advisors, mentors, and people who have achieved what you aspire to build. Continued education will be the secret sauce that enables you to keep growing and achieve your most significant financial goals.

Pick your brokerage account and a stockbroker. They will walk you through the process of opening an account, after which you can start investing in stocks and any other investment types available, depending on your financial situation and risk tolerance. Depending on how good your broker is and the services they offer you, that initial investment process can be enjoyable or quickly become a headache. You must do your due diligence before setting up a brokerage account and entering an agreement with any broker.

How Qualified Is Your Broker?

It's imperative to ensure you're dealing with a reputable broker before investing your hard-earned money. Do your homework well because there are plenty of scammers out there. Here are some ways you can check to ensure your broker is legit.

Do a Check with Professional Organizations.

You can check with professional and regulatory organizations to see where your broker stands. FINRA offers a database in their tool called Broker Check that can give you the stats on brokers and brokerages that agree to their standards. Everyone they verify will be on that list. If your broker isn't on that list, that can be okay, too, because only some are associated with FINRA (although it does help). In such a situation that what you want to do is make sure your broker meets fiduciary standards. The Securities and Exchange Commission (SEC) also has its database of registrations for the Series 65 license, which you can access through the Investment Adviser Public Disclosure page when you visit the SEC. So, find out what certifications and licenses your broker claims to have and then look them up on the appropriate sites.

Check Online

Google the broker's name and see what comes up on Google. If you come across their social media, this is a great place to visit what they are all about and what people think about their services in black and white. Many brokers and investment advisers are also required to register with their state. If your broker claims to be written, you can make a quick call to see if their information is valid and up to date.

Where to Find the Best Online Brokers.

If you want to find the best online brokers, an excellent resource to always bookmark is Investopedia. They continue to review and update the best-performing brokers as the market shifts. Some have been top-rated for years and enjoy the benefit of brand equity, which is why I include them in this book. However, I encourage keeping up to date by doing further research to see if any new ones are worthwhile. These are the most trusted and reputable brokers right now:

TD Ameritrade

TD Ameritrade is among the best options for beginners. Hence, I encourage you to visit their website first. They have $0 trade fees, $0 account minimum, and $0 annual or inactivity fees. You can get fabulous free research and a high-quality trading platform with excellent customer support.

Fidelity Investment

Fidelity Investments has a strong reputation for its mutual funds; however, it is considered one of the best and most rounded online brokers suitable for retirement investors and active traders. Fidelity offers $0 trading commissions, a $0 account minimum, and vital customer service. It has an easy-to-use platform and gives lots of research and educational materials.

TradeStation

Tradestation has $0 trade fees, a $0 account minimum, and comes with a high-quality trading platform. They also offer comprehensive research and other advanced tools to help you master your craft. This is a popular choice for stock, options, and futures investors.

Interactive Brokers

Interactive Brokers charge $0 trading fees with a $0 account minimum, and the best part is that they also offer international trade opportunities. The Lite version provides a quality trading platform and no stock-trading commissions. However, if you upgrade to the Pro version, there is an inactivity fee to pay.

Charles Schwab

Charles Schwab is excellent, whether you're a beginner or advanced. They offer $0 commissions, high-quality research, and a robust investment selection of no-transaction-fee mutual funds with low or no minimums. In addition to the basic trading capabilities offered by Charles Schwab, they also have several powerful trading platforms, all free and available to clients of all trading services.

Everything You Need To Know About Brokerage Accounts

You need a brokerage account to invest in the stock market. A brokerage account is a particular type of "account" like a bank account but different in that it enables you to buy and sell securities (e.g., bonds, mutual funds, stocks, forex, futures, etc.). Your stockbroker, whether discount or full service, should give you access to a brokerage account, and as you've seen above, many of them will allow you to set up an account with no minimum account obligations. The money you deposit into the brokerage account is what you'll use to purchase investments. It's good to know that you fully own the brokerage account and its assets as an investor. The broker is only an intermediary between you and the investments you want to purchase.

How brokerage accounts work and how to open one:

Once you feel ready to start your investment journey and know which brokerage Company to use, it's time to open your brokerage account. Opening an account is free and easy to do online in most cases.

All the recommended brokers I shared in this chapter allow you to open your brokerage account quickly in a few minutes. Then you can fund your account by transferring money from your checking or savings account - a process that can take a few days to a week, depending on your bank. The process is similar if you already have a brokerage account and want to move to something better now that you've read this book.

Once you sign up for the new account, you can transfer money from your old one to your new brokerage account. You often won't need a large sum to open a brokerage account. Some brokers need an initial deposit, while others don't ask for anything. Please get to know the policy with your new brokerage Company so you can organize your funds and allocate them accordingly. For example, if you go for a brokerage Company that requires an initial deposit of $1000, you need to transfer more than that amount to have money to purchase investments. Your broker should be able to walk you through this entire process to ensure everything is clear and manageable. If you're asked to choose between a cash account and a margin account, I encourage you to stick with a cash account first. A cash account is self-explanatory; you put cash in and use it to purchase. A margin account allows you to borrow money from the broker to make trades. As a newbie, this is never a good idea.

Many newbies always wonder if having more than one active brokerage account is a good idea, and the answer is yes and no. Go for it if you've got the money and can handle working with different brokerage accounts. There's no limit on the number of accounts you can have or how much money you can deposit into a taxable account annually.

Should you get a brokerage account or a retirement account?

The answer to that question depends on your investment goals. A brokerage account (a taxable account) has very few rules and restrictions. Although you have no tax advantages and your investment earnings will be taxed, you can move your money as you wish and invest as much as you'd like. If your main objective is retirement investing, a retirement account is a better way to go. You can open a retirement account such as a Roth or traditional IRA, granting you tax advantages. The catch to this is that you'll have restrictions around money movement. You can only withdraw and contribute money to such an account following guidelines, which your broker should help you clearly understand—more on this topic in the tax chapter.

What to Do with Broker Recommendations The jury is still out on this topic because some feel broker recommendations work, while others fear they don't. Many studies show that broker recommendations tend to be biased because they often favor companies with high cash flows, even if it comes from investments rather than business operations. They look for high price-to-earnings ratios etc. Going by these metrics alone could sometimes lead to shortcomings. Still, once you control for other variables, you'll find that stocks rated by analysts as buys tend to outperform those placed as sales during the subsequent one to six months. So, what does this mean for you? Use the research to understand the industry and the current operating environment. Know that forecasting on smaller stocks won't be as accurate as larger ones and give more importance to recent recommendations. Anything over three months old shouldn't be used to help you make an investment decision.

CHAPTER SIX

How To Utilize Time And The 8th Wonder Of The World

Time is tricky. If you have a good relationship with it, your investments can proliferate. However, it can also work against you if you don't learn to align your ambitions with the nature of things in the stock market world. How you utilize time once you become an investor will directly impact your success. In this chapter, we want to ensure you understand a few key concepts, all related to time.

The Waiting Game

Patience is a virtue. I'm sure you've heard that statement many times throughout life, and it holds even in this journey of becoming an elite investor. The waiting game is necessary and recommended if you want to do well as an investor. But it's not just waiting for the sake of staying.

Contrary to what most newbies think, it's not about waiting for the "whole market" to crash. Instead, the waiting game is strategic and very concentrated on a few key companies you've researched and feel confident will be your best investment. So it's not about "timing the market crash"; it's about following specific companies you believe in and knowing their total value. Then patiently waiting for the opportunity to take advantage of a temporary dip, those companies experience whether it affects the entire market.

Consider someone as successful as Warren Buffet, a master money-maker. Suppose we trace his actions and behavior as an investor. In that case, we can see that his strategies are excellently executed and tend to require tremendous research, knowledge, and patience. Warren often says that the priority (when it comes to investing) is to find cheap individual companies, ensure they have solid fundamentals, and go deep with those instead of focusing on investing in the market. His approach is simple yet requires much more work than you might think. It also requires playing the waiting game. Why? Because if you do your research, make your watchlist, and gather up your funds only to realize it's not the right time to invest, what should you do? Do you still purchase even when it's not a good deal? Of course not. As Buffet said, it's got to be a "sale."

Sales fall on your lap only a few times a week hence the importance of developing patience. You must wait until the right moment to act on that purchase. Some people assume that finding the right time is about predicting the market crash. Is that even possible? Can you envision a market crash? The truth is, predicting an impact is next to impossible. We are still determining when the next crash will be and what will trigger it. What we can do, however, is be prepared to act as soon as it occurs—based on observations and personal experience, waiting for those downtimes when the market dips are some of the best opportunities for an investor to purchase something that will yield a tidy profit.

Market Timing Vs. Buy and Hold

Buy-and-hold investing is the general term we use to refer to passive investing. It's when you purchase securities to hold for a long time. Long-term (depending on whom you ask) can be anything from three to a hundred years. On the other hand, market timing is actively investing and involves actively buying and selling. In this case, you aim to enter the market at the most advantageous time and get out before any meltdown or downfall occurs. Common sense tells us that market timing is challenging, and that's true.

According to current research, long-term buy-and-hold tends to outperform market timing investing. If you're the kind of investor wondering if you must choose one or the other, I have some good news. There's a strategy that combines both market timing and buy-and-hold methods within the same portfolio. With more education and professional help, you can combine active management with passive investing to maximize your return on both.

The 8th Wonder of The World

In this context, the eighth wonder of the world refers to the concept of compound interest. That is a topic few investors under- stand, and even fewer know how to make it work in their favor. Despite all my success and experience, I must confess that this concept wasn't clear for many years. It took a while before I grasped the importance of compound interest and how to make it work. For years I was making money but not capitalizing on this truth. I wasn't compounding my wealth, which resulted in linear growth instead of the alternative that compound interest can offer. What is compound interest? According to Investopedia, compound interest is interest calculated on the initial principal and the accumulated interest of previous periods of a deposit or loan. In other words, investing money should generate more money in the form of interest! So, as you invest and earn, that earned money starts to make money for you. How powerful is that? Compounding interest takes time. This is another waiting game because you won't see much action for the first twenty years. Things start getting exciting the longer you're in the game. In other words, the longer you're invested and the more you keep reinvesting, the more money you'll make from compounding. For example, many companies offer dividend reinvestment plans allowing you to reinvest cash dividends to purchase additional shares of stock. As you reinvest in more dividend-paying shares, your investor returns compound because the increased number of claims will consistently increase future income from dividend pay-outsΔ assuming the dividends remain stable. In such a case, you end up with "double compounding," which, over time, becomes a substantial number.

CHAPTER SEVEN

The Psychology Of Investing And The Mindset You Need

Winners think differently. It's that simple. If you want to be a successful investor, you've got to develop the kind of

mindset that all winners have. Many people skip over a chapter like this because they feel it's too "fluffy" or unimportant when investing. After all, investing and making money in the stock market is a game of logic, analysis, research, right choices, etc. And yes, that is true. But to assume your emotions don't factor into your decision-making and money-management abilities is to set yourself up for failure. So I commend you for reading this chapter to the end and putting some of the ideas you'll learn here into motion.

Here's the truth. You will need to work hard to succeed, and you'll also need to gain experience and mastery as you grow. The knowledge you continue to gain will make a difference in your performance as an investor. However, let me assure you that nothing will hinder or catapult your success in life more than how you think. That's why you must come to terms with your current mindset.

What is your current psychological state? Are you even aware of how you think, why you react in specific ways around money, etc.? Do you know what biases or beliefs you might have that subconsciously affect your decision-making process?

Putting Your Emotions on A Leash

A lack of control over emotions such as greed, pride, fear, anxiety, or anger may negatively impact the way you invest and, more importantly, the decisions you make concerning your investments. Having the right strategy, picking the right stock, and following your plan is fantastic, but it only sometimes works perfectly. Stock market investing requires someone who can play well in less-than-ideal situations. I recently met Steve at a conference where we were both guest speakers on investing. He shared how he learned this truth the hard way. Steve has always been a numbers guy, so he figured active investing would be easy. He considered himself very logical and did everything right by the book when he first got into investing. At first, things seemed to go well. He had a strong strategy, implemented it exceptionally well, and prided himself on always picking the best stocks. He was doing great for a young investor until the first significant correction in the share market came, and he started losing money. The only problem was that Steve was in love with the security that was going downhill. The beautiful portfolio he was carefully building up in record time started falling apart, and he lost it! As he watched the value of his investment fall, fear and anxiety crept in and overwhelmed him. It clouded his judgment and his ability to act fast. His pride got in the way because his ego couldn't accept what was happening, given how "perfect" his plan was. Studies have shown that people experience more pain in losing $1 than they would feel pleasure in gaining the same amount. Steve indeed fell into that category. The sting crippled him a lot, yet instead of selling to preserve capital, he held on to losing positions, and in the end, he got wiped out. What happened to Steve? His emotions hijacked his decision-making skills.

Steve is a very rational and logical guy. He studied, researched, and analyzed the stock market for two years before investing his first dollar. After getting into the game, he was chart reading and keeping up with the daily trends. Steve knew well what to do - when to cut losses, avoid bleeding out, etc. He knew everything, and yet he did none of it. We like to assume that investing and trading are rational processes, but we forget that our emotions influence behavior. Even if, in theory, you know what to do, if you don't take the time to understand better how you think, feel, and what drives your emotions and behavior, you might end up experiencing the same disaster that Steve had. I have shared this story with you as he did with the audience at that conference, hoping you will learn from this and prioritize mastery of your emotions.

The best way to avoid being ruled by emotions is to discipline your- self. Create a rules-based approach to investing once you determine what kind of investor you are, and then be disciplined enough to follow the rules you put in place. For example, you can decide not to change asset allocation due to recent market activity or select low-cost funds to represent asset classes in the budget. You can choose to only focus on long-term investment if that feels right for you; in this case, you can form a prudent asset allocation based on that decision that allows you to maintain that portfolio through all market conditions. Here are some tips to help you take emotions out of your investment even more. Avoid getting trapped by the minutia of daily stock trading. Unless you're an active day trader, looking at the minute-by-minute changes in the stock market and price fluctuations won't serve you very much. If anything, it will only breed fear, just as it happened for Steve. As both investor and an active trader, Steve could have taken a different course of action and made other choices. This advice is especially crucial for long-term investors. Don't feel the need to keep up with daily price fluctuations. Limited check-ins will lead to increased feelings of security and improved decision-making. Don't fall in love with your stocks. The stocks won't love you back, no matter how hard you try. Yes, it's hard to swallow your pride, admit you made a wrong decision, and sell the investment, but sometimes, that's the smart move. Emotions will try to take over and cloud your judgment. You might have all the right reasons in the world, but if it's not sound to hold on, make sure you sell that investment as fast as possible.

Put a stop loss on your investment by deciding when enough is enough. Once you cross that threshold, make sure you have parameters in place to help you execute the selling of that investment before you lose everything.

Seasonal Anomalies

In everyday communication, the term anomaly refers to abnormal behavior or occurrence. In the financial markets, however, we use this term to refer to any situation whereby a security or group of securities acts contrary to the notion of EMH (efficient market hypothesis). A great example of an anomaly that's famous occurred in 1987. October 19th of that year is considered a dark day and adequately coined "Black Monday" because a sudden and largely unexpected stock market crash started in Hong Kong and penetrated Europe and the United States of America. The collision was so severe that the Dow Jones Industrial Average dropped over 22% daily. Since then, the term Black Monday has been commonly used by critics to dismantle the efficient market hypothesis. Whenever the stock market deviates from that usual behavior, an anomaly occurs. There needs to be concrete proof to logically teach what anomalies are because they come and disappear with almost no warning (as the story above just showed). Some re-appear, while others never repeat themselves. At this point, we know that most stock market anomalies are psychologically driven, and although they can be great opportunities for you as an investor, make sure they don't dictate your trading decisions. Below I will share some common anomalies you might want to look for.

January Effect

Historically, stock prices tend to increase noticeably during the month of January. Several factors could influence this phenomenon, such as many investors usually selling off their losers in December. It could also be because investors like to use year-end bonuses to purchase new investments at the start of the year. I find this anomaly more rational than the others I'm about to share because it makes sense to cut writing the loss off your taxes.

Price Reversals

There is some supportive evidence that a reversal will occur in subsequent months when stocks perform well or poorly over 12 months. So, what am I saying? Yesterday's top performers might become tomorrow's underperformers and vice versa. Although there is some logic to this, understand that since most investors expect this shift to happen, it's probably bound to become a self-fulfilling anomaly. Unfortunately, predicting when investor sentiment or other factors trigger a price reaction is complex. Still, if you've seen a consistent rise in your winners for a long time, it might be time to re-evaluate how long you want to keep them.

Neglected Company Effect

Once you've played this game for a while, you might realize that most focus is on a specific set of companies—the more prominent players. Companies with smaller or relatively low balance sheet evaluations are often neglected and lack exposure. This causes them to be undervalued by the marketplace and makes them less visible to investors.

The days of the week are one of those anomalies that doesn't make much sense, and EMH supporters hate it the most. According to available research, stocks tend to move more on Fridays than Mondays. That has created a bias toward positive market performance on Fridays. Although it is statistically accurate, please don't assume it's predictable. It's sometimes also called the weekend effect and has been documented since the early 70s. So, I recommend you refrain from buying stocks on Monday because although this phenomenon is persistent, it still needs to be something to bank on. As with all the other mentioned anomalies, let them influence when appropriate but don't base your final decision on any of them.

Keep Calm and Invest

Stock investing is only for you if you expect to become a wealthy investor while surviving any marketplace challenges. Volatility is the nature of the beast in stock market investing, and anyone who has built a healthy portfolio can tell you there will always be turbulence. For those who have only been investing for the past few years, their marketplace experience is lacking because they haven't weathered any big storms. The real test of a successful investor or trader is different from how much money they could make in the last twelve months. Instead, it's how many market crashes and downturns they have survived. Although we've had a few minor bumps (such as the end of 2018, wherein just four months, Nasdaq fell more than 23% impacting stocks like Apple, Amazon, and Netflix), none of these have been major hits. So, let me save you some Aspirin money or medical bills in advance with this solid advice: You must train yourself to stay calm and composed as an investor no matter what's going on in the marketplace. The most robust and most successful investors I know manage to keep their calm even when the market tanks. Want a few ideas to help you do the same?

Plan

This isn't rocket science. I just told you there's no way a good investor won't experience volatility. So make sure you have a contingency plan ahead of time. If you're prepared for the inevitable market crash, you'll be more robust, calmer, and capable of making the right moves. Stop obsessing about your portfolio or what the daily charts are telling you.

If you are a real stock investor (which I assume you have read this far), then you know our game is the long-term play. As such, you must limit how often you check stock charts or your portfolio when things are going awry. This is good for your mental and emotional health and finances because you'll avoid impulsive decisions.

Back Test

Trends are constantly repeating themselves. It's easy to gain perspective when you review long-term trends and other historical records because it can help you see that stock-market corrections always work themselves out in the long run.

Ground yourself in your "Why."

Simon Sinek made the concept of "start with your why" popular in the leadership space. I want you to adopt some of that thinking to your investment because you are the leader of your stock investment business. And beyond just knowing your "why," I also want you to remind yourself of it whenever you get anxious or too caught up in the game. Investing can give us such a rush and sometimes become overwhelming. Keep yourself grounded, and you'll remain calm.

Keep Investing

This might sound wild and counterintuitive to most readers. Still, the truth is that whenever there's a downturn or market correction, an excellent opportunity lurks amid that chaos. Warren Buffet told Fortune Magazine not too long ago that he's a big fan of buying more when others pull out. "The lower things go, the more I buy," said Buffet. Of course, that means you must have a sound mind, a solid long-term plan, and the right mental state to make this work. This book is already preparing you to be ready. For such opportunities, if you implement everything, you learn.

For some, even with all the knowledge and planning, it might not be a good idea to risk further when volatility is high, which brings me to my next important point. Do you know your personality, temperament, and mindset well enough to pick investment styles that work in your favor?

What Kind of Investor Are You?

Here are the various types of investors experts have identified. See if any of these traits resonate with you so you can improve your chances of winning with your investment strategies.

Automatic Investor

This type of investor cares a lot about convenience. They prefer to have everything on autopilot and take a hands-off investing approach. If this is more your type, you're looking for solutions enabling you to automatically contribute to your investment funds by directly transferring funds from your bank account on a particular day of each month. You want the ability to sit back, relax, and focus on other things as your investment efforts work in the background automatically. You can automate your investments, especially if you choose a full-service broker who will often help automate the process and align you with the best buys and strategies that match your needs and objectives.

A significant advantage of this approach is that you don't have to micro-manage or daily monitor the volatility of your investments since most of them will grow over many years. You can avoid the anxiety that most investors and traders experience. Things like compounding interest should be of great interest to you.

A disadvantage of being this type of investor is that you may need complete control of your investment portfolio. If you lose touch with where your investment funds are going and how your portfolio performs, it might harm you in the long run. That is especially true if you rebalanced your portfolio infrequently to ensure you're getting rid of the depreciating assets.

Conscientious Investor

This investor only gets involved with companies that align with their values and moral principles. It goes beyond just making money or building a portfolio. If you're this type of investor, it's more about investing in socially or environmentally responsible companies. An advantage of being a conscientious investor is your impact and influence on others and the world as you demonstrate what you stand for and who you are through the types of companies you promote and invest in.

Unfortunately, this can also create certain limitations, resulting in lower returns. But given that you're driven by impact and a particular moral code, even that limitation may not necessarily be a disadvantage in my eyes because some things are worth more than money. And if you just resonated with that notion, perhaps this is your investor type, so take time to pick your stocks and ensure the companies you invest in align with your values.

Property Investor

This type of investor is more interested in building a portfolio that deals with familiar and easy-to-control assets. They own gold, maybe even bonds, collectibles, or real estate. If you're this investor, you care about putting your money into things you understand. The idea of Wall Street and dealing with constant market volatility is highly unsettling. So, after learning in this book how stock investing works, you might opt for a different type of investment that feels more stable, such as real estate. That's why, earlier in this book, I shared the different types of assets available to you. You don't have to invest in stocks to become financially independent. I have many friends who only invest in real estate, and they've built much wealth around that.

I encourage people to follow in my footsteps and start with stocks because I've experienced first-hand the rich benefits of this type of investing. Compared to other investment types, stock investing offers excellent returns in a relatively short time, so don't just shy away from the opportunity because it's the unknown. An advantage of becoming this type of investor is that you will be exposed to less volatility than a stock investor.

The huge disadvantage is the missed opportunity of the enormous returns of stock investing. Large-cap value stocks are a relatively safe way to start your investment journey if you want to play it safe.

Bargain Investor

The bargain investor is an intriguing type. They are always searching for bargain deals, which is fun if you like that kind of hunting. And in many cases, if you know what you're doing, you can create some big wins. If you're this type of investor, then stocks that cost $1 per share appeal to you. Penny stocks are where you like to invest your time because you see the potential and enjoy watching that penny turn into a pretty profit. Of course, there's always the risk that those bargain stocks could become worthless- but you feel it's worth taking. It's about carefully assessing the P/E ratios to check the share price relative to earnings per share before picking which stock to invest in.

As we've seen with many investors who've made millions from bargain deals, a considerable advantage of this is that you can strike big. The disadvantage, however, is that these low bargain prices could easily dupe you. Sometimes the fees are trading at low prices for a good reason. If you can sort out the fakers from the real bargain deals, you should be able to do well in the long run.

Daily Dow Watcher

This type of investor is current with what's trending up or down. They are up to speed, know the current market price, know how much their portfolio is worth at any given time, continuously monitor stock charts, etc. If the market has a bad day, this type of investor immediately stresses out and might get tempted to sell out.

A significant advantage of being this type of investor is that you're always up to speed with the current trends of the marketplace. Unfortunately, keeping tabs on the market can also be a source of frustration and anxiety because the stock market is highly volatile. If you're always on your smartphone checking daily charts, you'll get stressed and discouraged and might impulsively decide to sell stock out of fear when prices drop. By the way, selling your stock when prices drop (like most people do when a market drops) is almost always one of the worst moves an investor can make. Be informed but regulate it. Check on the stock market and your investment portfolio frequently (I suggest quarterly), and you'll be more productive and profitable.

Active Trader

If you're an investor who enjoys being an active trader, following the markets daily is a good idea. Investing and trading are not synonymous because not all investors can be profitable traders, and vice versa. Investing is a long-term game, whereas trading is usually a short-term game. Few are naturally gifted at both, and even if you can balance these two, you'd still need a massive amount of continued education to be great at both. Assuming you are great at both, then things get very exciting. This is where you play for the little wins and the long-term gains. Diversification is your ally. You want to be able to time the market correctly. And remember what I said. It's not about predicting when the market will crash. Instead, it's about taking the right action and buying suitable securities at a great price point when the crash happens. When others pull out, you pull the "buy" trigger strategically. To perform optimally, you need to buy an undervalued stock for whatever reason before other investors realize it, then sell it when it's near the peak price before most investors know it's going down. This execution will require you to immerse yourself in the market and economic data, business articles, financial reports, etc. You've got to know your stuff because none of it is guesswork. Your risk appetite must be high as well.

An advantage of being this type of investor is that you can enjoy unlimited success, especially when you get the timing right. The disadvantage is the loss you can incur. Trading fees can also get expensive if your investment approach requires making many trades, so tread carefully.

Portfolio Tweaker

This type of investor isn't actively trading. However, they enjoy frequently updating and fine-tuning their portfolio by transferring funds to get the desired balance between large-cap, mid-cap, small-cap, growth, foreign, domestic, value, and bond investment categories.

An advantage of being this type of investor is that it's easier to keep track of your progress and meet your investment goals. Please do it effectively because sometimes it might hurt your overall return. A good habit to get into is to rebalance your portfolio at most twice a year, especially if you're a relatively new investor.

Company Loyalist

This type of investor is loyal to a specific brand. They go into the stock market game, knowing exactly which company they want to pour most of their money (if not all) into. Often, it's a company they work for already or a trendy brand that inspires loyalty, such as Apple, Tesla, etc. This kind of loyalty can be advantageous because if the company does well, you'll do well.

The main disadvantage I see if you're this type of investor is that you make yourself vulnerable in the marketplace because of your need for more diversification. I've mentioned this a few times in this book and often remind my students that lack of diversification is hazardous. Putting all your eggs in one basket (even if you'd take a bullet for that brand) is not a wise move as a stock investor.

The Winning Mindset

You must work on your mindset to become a successful investor and build wealth quickly. The rules of making money as a stock investor are easy to understand and, with practice, get easier to execute. The one thing that doesn't naturally occur is emotional maturity. You've got to have tremendous mental discipline and a good handle on emotions like fear, greed, laziness, and pride if you want to succeed. An expert study reports that less than 10% of investors are rich after learning the right strategies. Why do you think that is?

I'll save you some thinking time - it's primarily because most people cannot manage their emotions and have no idea how to develop a winning mindset.

How you think about stock market investing and your emotional relationship with money will make all the difference in the world. Many new investors must correct the mistake of treating stock investing as a hobby. They think of stocks in very trivial ways. Some- times it does help to see the stock market mechanically and concha- lately because it takes the emotion out of it. But instead of downplaying the stock market to protect your feelings, how about taking a different approach? I encourage you to think of yourself as part-owner of the company you invest in. By assuming that, you become focused on the things that matter. As an owner of several businesses now, I am always thinking long-term. I don't make hasty decisions and dive into more excellent details when analyzing situations. This is a habit I also bring to my investment decisions, and it has helped me tremendously.

Another mental shift I want you to make concerns how much you need to diversify. I know you've heard, "Never put your eggs in one basket," which is true. However, I also know that being over-diversified can hurt your growth. To avoid being overstretched in any one way, invest significantly in a handful of companies. Instead of a broad yet weak portfolio, consider building a narrower portfolio with a few stable investments of good companies that show excellent growth prospects. Remember, the most successful investors do their due diligence, take their time to dig deep into a company, and go with their "gut." If you've done all the necessary research and you "feel" it's a good deal - take the chance.

CHAPTER EIGHT

Technical and Fundamental Analysis of The Stock Market

There are two main disciplines that every stock investor and trader should know if they want to do well in this industry.

These are the two main methods used to study, measure, and judge market behavior. Both are essential for us to learn as stock investors as they make forecasting easier and identify trends. These studies estimate both the short-term and long-term value of the market. Given their proven reliability, you can use these two methods in almost any investment category, so it will benefit you to learn as much as you can about each of these over the coming months. What am I referring to? Technical and fundamental analysis, of course. While this book doesn't offer a complete and comprehensive course on either (for that, I recommend taking up an online course on Udemy), it will give you the basics needed to start practicing as soon as today. The better you understand and utilize technical and fundamental analysis, the easier it will be to make informed decisions as you begin investing.

What is the main objective of doing any analysis?

To determine the current price of the stock you want to invest in is reasonable. As you branch more plunging into the two methods, a few variations arise because each analysis focuses on different aspects and time length, but the bottom line always stays the same. They are tools to ensure you get into a good deal for short-term or long-term gains. Let's dissect the main differences between Technical and Fundamental analysis to ensure everything is clear.

The Difference Between Technical and Fundamental Analysis

Fundamental analysis is a method stock investor use to evaluate a company by determining the intrinsic value of its stock. In other words, with the fundamental analysis, you would be digging into the annual and quarterly figures of the company, studying their management, competitors, and the economy trying to get at the company's actual value to determine if you want to invest your money there.

The technical analysis concerns the actual stock price or volume data and nothing else. The balance sheet of a company or how excellent the management is will bear no significance because this type of method is more concerned with identifying trading opportunities that can produce gains in the short term. So, in other words, the price action is what counts, not the underlying economics that affects the value of a company.

It's best not to ask which method is better when clarifying these two approaches (especially as newbies). Different investors will give you different answers. Some investors swear by technical analysis, while others only work with fundamental analysis. A keen investor needs to know and utilize both methods for optimum results. You may look at the difference between these two in the following way: Technical analysis is concerned with price action, which gives clues as to the stock's supply and demand dynamics in the marketplace. That determines the stock price and when it's an excellent time to buy. The focus there is price and volume data.

On the other hand, fundamental analysis concerns a company's value. It's about identifying the value of its assets and the profits it can generate. The focus is knowing the difference between a stock's underlying value and the current price at which it's trading in the marketplace. Short-term price movements are always determined by supply and demand in the market, which are, in turn, affected by more than what you'd find as you dig into the fundamental analysis. You can only analyze market sentiment and the effect of emotion on market activity through price and volume data.

On the other hand, regardless of how detailed your charts are, it's impossible to determine whether a stock is genuinely under or over-valued. And you certainly cannot forecast or predict any company's value years into the future. Hence, while charts are excellent for reflecting on what has happened in the past, they aren't that valuable when you're looking to make decisions about your future.

Tools to use for fundamental and technical analysis:

The company's financial statement is the most important data source for fundamental analysis. You need to understand the company's current financial health, such as the company's income statement, balance sheet, cash flow statements, etc. Does the company have debt? You need to know this. Have they recently changed management? That should matter to you. With all this information, you can calculate ratios and metrics that reflect the company's performance, health, and growth rates. You intend to arrive at and determine what is fair value. You can only do that by comparing several models and ratios.

Technical analysis requires charts. The main tools used in this analysis method are chart reading, including price charts (line charts, candlestick charts, bar charts, etc.) and various other indicators such as oscillators, price patterns, and complex analysis frameworks like Elliot Waves. As you can see, technical analysis is quite broad and highly complicated.

Which one should you focus on?

Again, I reiterate my statement from before. There is no right or wrong because it's not a binary answer. It depends on the type of investor you are and what your objectives are. Why would you be reading this book as an intelligent investor, which I assume you are otherwise? I will study both. Why? Because

Fundamental analysis is extremely useful for long-term investments, which we said is the main game with stock investing. Technical analysis is also instrumental when doing things like market timing and short-term trading, which many of my students get into to make some money in the short term as they also build their portfolios. So, combining both is a winning strategy if you want to be an investor who is also actively trading. Therefore, instead of telling you which one is better, let me aid you in approaching this smartly.

How to Use Fundamental and Technical Analysis Together in Stock Investing

A practical implementation of what we just discussed is to start by building a watchlist of stocks you're prepared to own based on the fundamental analysis you've conducted. Once you have your list, use technical analysis to decide if or when to buy them. Next, you should look at a price chart to get an idea of the direction of a trend. This will help you determine whether the market agrees with your valuation. Have a stronger conviction when going against the crowd and be prepared to exit quickly if a stock is widely owned and the fundamentals change.

You can also use fundamental research to determine which parts of a business cycle are most profitable for a company and then use technical analysis to confirm anticipated trends.

Another way to combine both is to use technical analysis to find good entry levels for growth stocks in an uptrend. Companies with high growth rates and trade on high valuations often experience significant corrections. In such cases, your technical analysis can be used to identify oversold levels, which is an excellent opportunity to buy growth stocks.

Trading Is Better for The Short Term in The Stock Market.

Have you ever heard of day trading? It's a trendy style of trading for short-term investing that earns you money over a short period. In other words, it's fast returns and typically very liquid. It's one of the most attractive ways to make money on the Internet today and perhaps one of the main reasons you picked up this book. You can buy and sell shares through day trading, earning a profit to achieve immediate gains. And yes, anyone can become a day trader. It works by finding good deals you can quickly enter and exit to achieve a high return in the shortest timeframe possible. Sometimes you enter and exit trades within a matter of minutes. Yes, it can get intense and exciting. Your ability to exercise patience and, at the same time, be quick to act determines how well you do in any given trade. Let me be clear here. Day trading will not build your investment portfolio. It's not meant to play that game. Day trading is about earning you money, giving you a source of income in the short term if you need it, and much of that hinges on your ability to get rid of shares fast.

The price movement that continually goes up and down throughout the trading day (hour by hour) is what you're monitoring because that's where your profit lies. As you might have guessed, this game is more about psychology than numbers. Numbers play a minimal role in day trading. You need a good trading strategy that you must learn and develop to suit your personality and master; then, you must implement it religiously. There is no wiggle room, and you must follow your trading plan. That's where your mindset makes a difference. If you want to go down this path, I encourage you to further your education by studying day trading for beginners.

Investing Is Better for The Long Term in The Stock Market

The whole purpose of stock investing is to build something profitable long-term. That's where the real money is. Even though day trading makes you money, it must differ from what you can create for yourself with long-term investments. A healthy portfolio is a mix of mid to long-term investments, but as Warren Buffet evangelizes, the main aim should always be going as long as possible because that makes all the difference. Long-term investments always do well despite market fluctuations, downturns, recessions, and volatility. If you can weather the storms of the marketplace, then you will win. One of the main advantages of this type of investing is that dividends and compound interest become very attractive and plausible. We already mentioned the benefits involved in both earning rewards and being able to compound your interests. The psychology you need is also different.

When making long-term investments, you typically run a much

smaller risk of losing money on the stock market, and you don't need to concern yourself much with the daily drama of the marketplace. If you choose a great broker who can offer you reasonable transaction costs and who helps you set up the correct account for your preferred investing style, you should be good to go - no stress, just a lot of patience. If you invest your money long-term, go as long as possible (preferably 20 years or more). To be confident that this will pay off in the end, use everything we've discussed in this book so far, don't shortcut your research, and above all else, go for companies you genuinely feel will appreciate over time.

CHAPTER NINE

How to Buy Stocks and Deal with Recession

Now that you understand how to use fundamental and technical analysis and combine them in your stock investing business, it's time to apply these lessons. Using what you've learned, you will now be able to choose the right stock, and in this chapter, I want to assist you in doing so. Afterward, I'll also share some insights to help you deal with the inevitable market downturn,

crashes, and even possible recession so that you're always prepared.

How to choose the right stock.

By now, you should realize that selecting a good stock to build your portfolio must begin with an in-depth study of the company's fundamentals. In other words, you need to become a fundamental analyst. The goal is to ensure that the stock you invest in is worthwhile. And to help you spot any red flags you need to become aware of before taking the plunge. An excellent place to start is by researching companies you already know, whether you've used them as a consumer or read about them for years in financial papers etc. By now, you should already have your brokerage account and ample know-how on implementing the fundamental and technical analysis you've learned in this book. It would be best to have an investment plan with a clear strategy. If you apply everything you've learned and have an excellent broker to assist you, picking your first stock to fit your investing needs should be easy. If your due diligence allows you to go ahead and buy the stock, decide how many shares you want to buy.

How Much Does It Cost and How Much Should You Buy

The cost of becoming a stock investor will vary significantly based on various factors, many of which we've discussed. Factors include what broker you'll choose, which type of investment style you'll go for, how many shares you'll buy etc. There are no stiff or rigid rules for investing here. You can invest as little or as much as your financial situation (and investment account) allows. The two main factors when it comes to stock price are the price of the stock itself and the fee (commission) your broker charges. A young company still in its early stages of an initial public offering (IPO) can only be purchased on the primary market and is usually set by the issuing entity. This price is fixed and non-negotiable. Suppose you want to play in the secondary market to buy a company not in the early IPO stage. In that case, the price isn't predetermined by the issuing entity or fixed, as it varies depending on the market psychology. As for the commissions, it depends on whom you work with. Some charge a flat fee; others charge a percentage of the total trade value, etc.

In some cases, there will also be other extra costs associated with having a brokerage account, so you want to consider all these things when deciding on your initial investment, but suppose you go for a reputable online broker such as TD Ameritrade. You know they charge no fees for account minimums, and opening an account is quick and easy, so you can begin your investment journey with as little as $500 and grow it as you grow. The cost of the stock you buy will also vary. If you go into penny stock trading, you can buy way more shares with a $500 investment compared to buying Netflix or Amazon shares. So, make sure your ambitions match your finances.

Buying Your First Stock

I recommend you start as small as possible. Dip your toes into the water and get a taste of what it's like to own shares before diving into the deep end of the ocean with the sharks. Instead of pouring all your money in at once to fill your entire portfolio, make your first purchase of a single share of a company you feel convinced will do well. If you have the skill, mental and emotional stability, and strength to ride through the rough patches that might arise without losing your mind, then start adding to your portfolio over time as you continue to educate yourself.

Recession and How to Take Advantage of The Situation

Nothing hurts the economy and, in turn, companies and the stock market more than a recession. A recession is a slowdown or a significant halt to the economic growth of a country. There have been numerous recessions in the past, the biggest one being the great recession that ended in 2009. That created much devastation in the marketplace as people sold off their assets in panic. While it can be devastating to find yourself in the middle of an economic meltdown (which no one can ever predict accurately), it's not all doom and gloom. Going through a recession can work in your favor if you don't panic and create a contingency plan. The first lesson you must learn about a recession is that it won't last forever. And once it's over, the investors that weather the storm and stay strong usually come out on top because the market always recovers after a recession.

There are a few things you can start doing whenever you notice the market is beginning to show signs of decline. You can take advantage of a declining market through the dollar-cost averaging method discussed earlier in the book. Go back and read that section if you can't recall. Another thing you can do is diversify your portfolio by purchasing dividend stocks through mutual funds or exchange-traded funds that only invest in dividend-paying companies. More on what ETFs are later.

Investing in consumer staples is the best possible strategy for surviving a recession. What are consumer staples? Think of companies like Walmart, Proctor & Gamble, etc. Even if the economy is down, families still must spend money on food supplies, medicine, hygiene products, etc. They may not buy cars, televisions, or other luxury products, but they'll undoubtedly continue to shop for necessities. The more you can invest in such companies, the better off you'll be during a market downturn.

Recently U.S.News shared an article with the seven stocks that have historically soared even during a recession. According to their report, the stocks that held up during the 2008 recession were Hasbro (HAS), Ross Stores (ROST), Walmart (WMT), Amgen (AMGN), Anheuser Busch InBev (BUD), H&R Block (HBR), and Dollar Tree (DLTR). You're familiar with some, if not all, of these companies. In the report, we are told that when many dividend stocks were slashing to ceasing payments altogether, Walmart managed to grow its earnings per share and even increase its dividend by 8%. This leads me to my second important lesson about a recession. If you're going to hold stocks during a recession, the best ones to own are the ones that demonstrate much resilience. A company that is established and has a strong balance sheet and cash flow. I'm a huge fan of consumer staples because if you choose the right ones, you'll get a nice cushion during the crash and emerge even more significant than before, assuming you apply the right strategy.

CHAPTER TEN

The Easiest Way To Make Your Investment Strategy Passive And Grow Long-Term (Index Funds And Etfs)

There are dozens of ways to get passive income. Of course, this is every investor's dream, and regardless of how you plan on doing it, the two main elements needed to turn that dream into reality will always be time and money. You need to have time or money to make it work. Most people starting this game have neither. Suppose you've got much money already but need more time to generate passive income. But if you're starting from scratch with little or no money, you'll have to invest much time initially before you can reap the rewards later. The most vital component of creating passive income is honesty, assessing where you are, and putting in as much effort as needed without wavering until things snowball. For some, it might mean working late into the night. For others, it might mean cutting out on too many social get-togethers or binge-watching Netflix on weekends. Unless you can make the sacrifice, that dream of passive income will remain a wish.

As an investor, you can focus on being passive or active. Do you know what the difference is between these two terms? Let's clarify.

Passive Investing Vs. Active Investing

Passive investing is more about automating and being hands-off with your investments because you intend to do it for the long haul. This is the classic buy-and-hold approach, which we've discussed throughout this book. As the name implies, active investing means you're very involved in managing your portfolio. The goal is to beat the stock market's average returns and take advantage of short-term price fluctuations. Therefore, you need to be deeply immersed in technical analysis and learn to predict as much as possible market timing. You can succeed as an active investor if you can be more right than wrong. However, if you're not interested in playing that intense game of chasing the latest trends and price movements, then you'll be best taking on a passive investor role. Have someone else manage your portfolio. Passive investing is straightforward, and you always know which assets are in an index fund. The fees are low, and it's very tax efficient. A downside to this type of investing is that your returns will be low since you're not actively trying to beat the market or get the most significant profits. Passive funds are also limited to a specific index or predetermined set of investments with little to no variation.

On the other hand, active investing is flexible, and you have complete control over your portfolio and its investments. You can hedge your bets and sell off the losers to offset taxes on the big winners. One of the disadvantages of being an active investor is that the risks are much higher. It also comes with costly fees because of all the buying and selling involved, which incurs transaction fees and commissions. Over time, those fees can eat up your returns and profits to the point where it makes no sense to maintain your portfolio, so be intentional with whichever path you choose. Both styles are beneficial, but one might be more favorable depending on your personality and investing objectives. Aside from direct (single) stock investing, there are other investments you can add to your portfolio to continue building wealth. Here are three types.

Index Funds

An index fund is a mutual fund - a collection of stocks, bonds, or other types of securities that tracks a market index (e.g., S&P 500). Before you can understand what, an index fund is, you need to understand the definition of an index.

According to my knowledge, the word index is a made-up concept. An academic idea that's been accepted by the masses and the marketplace. It's a person or a committee sitting down and creating a list of rules for constructing a portfolio of individual holdings. For example, one of the oldest index funds is the Dow Jones Industrial Average, a list of thirty blue chip stocks selected by The Wall Street Journal editors. The list comprises a representative collection of stocks that are important to the economy of the United States, and they are weighted based on the stock price. Instead of having a portfolio manager making selections with an index fund, you outsource the capital allocation job to the individual or committee determining the index methodology.

How do they work?

Index funds are managed by fund managers who make sure the fund tracks the underlying index. They can be structured in two primary ways: Index mutual funds (offered directly through mutual fund companies) and index exchange-traded funds (these trade now on stock exchanges). If you own index exchange-traded funds with your brokerage account, you can easily buy or sell shares at any point when the stock market is open for trading.

Exchange-Traded Funds (ETF)

An exchange-traded fund is a basket of securities you can buy and sell through your brokerage Company on a stock exchange. This can be stocks, bonds, commodities, or a combination.

ETFs have become extremely popular because they have the diversification benefits mutual funds offer while simultaneously mimicking the ease with which stocks are traded. You can buy market ETFs that track a particular index like the S&P 500, bond ETFs, commodity ETFs that track the price of commodities such as oil, gold, or corn, foreign market ETFs, Inverse ETFs designed to profit from a decline in the underlying market or index and so much more.

How does it work?

ETFs work like a company stock during the day when the stock exchanges are open. An ETF has a ticker symbol, and intraday price data is readily accessible during trading. The number of shares outstanding in an ETF can change daily (unlike a company stock), and this is due to the continuous creation of new shares and the redemption of existing shares. The market price of ETFs generally stays in line with their underlying securities because of the ETF's ability to issue and redeem shares continuously. ETFs are popular with investors because you can buy and sell them any time of the day, you have better control over capital gains tax, and because they are traded like stocks, you can place various orders. The fees are also relatively low as there is no sales load. You only need to worry about the regular commission to your broker.

As with all investments, some drawbacks come with investing in ETFs, including technical issues while tracking an underlying index. This can create unfortunate discrepancies. Some thinly traded ETFs also have a wide bid/ask spread, which means you might buy high and sell low. If you invest in small amounts regularly, there may be better solutions than this, as there are other lower-cost alternatives for investing directly with a fund company in a no-load fund.

Dividend Investing

If you have been reading this book looking for a proven system to help you build wealth primarily through passive income generation and were wondering when I would spill the beans - this is it right here. I have seen this method work for myself and countless others. This is the surest investing strategy that can create a passive income but can be challenging. It can be done.

Dividend investing, which we discussed in an earlier chapter, is very straightforward. The only thing you need to make this system work for you is a good understanding of what dividend investing is and how it works, and you need the mindset to execute. That means you must be patient because dividends only work if you use a long-term approach. You need to invest in companies that pay dividends. Start with one or as many as your finances permit, then add to your portfolio as your income grows. When you receive your payout, don't just spend it on stuff. Instead, it would be best to reinvest it to purchase more shares to build a profitable and secure portfolio in the long haul (more than ten years later). Let me repeat - the main objective is to buy shares that pay dividends and hold on to them as long as possible. It is a long-term investment that earns you money as the years roll on.

What about diversification?

Diversifying your investments is always a good idea, and it's no different here. I recommend purchasing from other companies and even sectors whenever possible.

CHAPTER ELEVEN

Tax Protected Investments

There's a lot to learn when you're getting started on your investing journey, and most of the time, we tend to neglect the topic of taxes, mainly because of how overwhelming and confusing the issue is. So, it's understandable if you feel tempted to skip over this chapter. However, I encourage you to resist that temptation because understanding how taxes work will save you many headaches. Death and taxes are inevitable; you've heard that saying. I encourage you to avoid death at all costs. But regarding taxes, a little knowledge on how to best manage will prove wise for your peace of mind and wealth-building efforts.

Tax System On Your Investments

You can only grow your stock investments if you understand the tax basics on ordinary income, capital gains, and capital losses because these affect your investment strategy. The most important thing to know as a new investor is that here in the

United States, you only pay taxes on investments that increase in value if you sell them. Also, the holding period matters when calculating capital gains taxes because long-term investments are subject to lower tax rates.

Ordinary income

Ordinary income investment profit is taxed at the same rate as wages. Depending on your tax bracket, you can calculate how much tax you need to pay. The two types of investments that fall into this category are dividends and short-term capital gains. So, if your tax bracket is 28%, then that's the rate at which your dividends and short-term capital gains will be taxed. For tips, some exceptions occur depending on whether they happen in a tax-sheltered plan such as a 401(K) or an IRA and whether they fall under the "qualified dividends" type, a dividend receiving preferential tax treatment. Be sure to check with your accountant for exactly what applies to you.

Regarding short-term capital gains, this applies to stocks you've sold for a profit (that you owned for a year or less). To calculate whether the stock falls into this category, you must use the trade date (date of execution), not the settlement date. Again, even with this scenario, you might be exempt from taxes if the gains occur in a tax-sheltered plan.

Long-term capital gains

This occurs when you sell an investment at a profit you've held for over a year. The gains are taxed according to the IRS's long-term capital gains tax rates depending on your total taxable income (0%, 15%, 20%). In addition, if you fall into the category of the higher-income taxpayer, you might also have to pay a 3.8% net investment income tax, which applies to any investment income (e.g., interest income, rental income from real estate, dividends, etc.) In short, long-term capital gains receive more favorable tax treatment. Also, they offer different ways to manage and control your tax burden. A conversation with your accountant and financial planner should help you understand your income bracket and the advantages available to you.

How To Pay Lower Taxes on Stocks

The easiest way to do this is by thinking long-term instead of short-term. Consider holding an asset for at least a year, preferably more, as that will qualify you for a long-term capital gains tax rate when you sell. As mentioned, long-term capital gains taxes are much lower than short-term capital gains taxes. You might pay less tax on your dividends by holding the shares long enough for the rewards to count as qualified dividends. This doesn't mean solely focusing on the long-term. Be intentional about the stocks you buy and the type of account you open to ensure everything aligns with your investment goals and works in your favor.

There are two types of investment accounts. Depending on your choice, you will be exposed to certain drawbacks and advantages regarding taxation. The two models are taxable accounts and tax-advantaged accounts. In this book, we've primarily focused on a taxable account (a brokerage account is a taxable account). Taxable accounts are outstanding because they have more flexibility, offer few restrictions, and you can withdraw your money anytime for any reason with no penalty or tax. However, they have no tax benefits. Tax advantage accounts such as a 401(k) or an IRA are usually tax-exempt or tax-deferred. However, you do pay taxes when you withdraw your money, and you also don't have the flexibility or freedom to move your money as you like because they come with specific fixed rules. For example, in 2020, you can contribute $6000 to your IRAs or $7000 if you're 50 or older. With a 401(k), you can contribute up to $19,500 or up to $26,000 if you're 50 or older. It's great that you don't get taxed upfront with such accounts. It is wise to hold all your investments in a tax-advantaged account. Still, given the limitations, I need help finding it efficient. That's why I've focused purely on a brokerage account.

Depending on your investment goals, you need to figure out what the best solution will be. A good rule of thumb when deciding what would be the "right account" is to keep those investments that lose less of their returns to taxes on a taxable account. Then the ones that could lose a lot of the profit on taxes, I suggest putting those into a tax-advantaged account.

How To Protect Your Investments

The best way to protect your investment is to educate yourself on money management and get a qualified accountant who can assist you in understanding your tax situation because it will be different for everyone. Then I encourage you to contact a taxable and tax-advantaged account, as most intelligent investors have both. Allocate the right assets to the preferred accounts (as suggested in the last paragraph). For example, I would put individual stocks I plan to hold for longer than a year into a brokerage account and wait for them to qualify for long-term capital gains. Then individual stocks meant for the short term (less than a year) would go right into my IRA or 401 (k). In other words, whenever I actively manage stock funds that generate short capital gains, my go-to account would be the tax-advantaged one. Then as I diversify and grow my portfolio with index funds, ETFs, etc., those would mainly be on my taxable account. Makes sense? The more you can minimize your taxes, the better off you'll be. Everyone will have a unique situation depending on their income bracket, whether you apply as a single or married couple, etc. So, this is meant to give you only some of the details you need, but it does give you an overview and a starting point in this often-overwhelming topic. Now, make an appointment to see a qualified financial advisor or tax professional so you can choose the best tax strategy for your goals and current situation.

CHAPTER TWELVE

Investing Your Way to Complete Financial Freedom and Early Retirement

---

If you want to achieve financial freedom and build enough want to achieve financial freedom and build enough wealth that enables you to retire whenever you desire, you've got to make it happen. It takes effort, a lot of intention, commitment, and discipline most people aren't willing to deploy. Having read this far, you're different from most people. You are determined to design and live your life on your terms. It's a very noble decision, and you sure deserve it. So let me be honest with you. The way to achieve complete financial freedom and early retirement is to learn these three things:

First, you need to get good at making money. That includes your current job or business and the investments you will make in the stock market.

Second, you need a plan to help you keep this money. You can only save money when you know how to manage, budget, and make it work for you, which leads me to my last tip.

Third, you need to know how to multiply your well-managed money so it can go to work for you and make you wealthy.

If you can focus on those three key steps, you will find yourself in that elite club of financially independent men and women who get to travel the world, do what they love, and live life on their terms. I assume you're already good at making money and earning an income. This book has just introduced you to the best way to take your current cash and use it to build wealth. But it wouldn't be a complete book if I didn't help you think through the plan of how you'll make your investments work for you. To do that, let's talk about your investment plan.

Creating an Investing Budget

If you want financial freedom and early retirement to become a reality, you must set the right goals. It would be best to have short, intermediate, and long-term goals leading to that bigger picture.

With your short-term goals, you want to think about and embrace having a tight budget that you always live by. Then you want to start planning an emergency fund. These are relatively easy things to do if you stay disciplined and committed. For your budget, you need the following:

- Non-discretionary expenses. These include rent, insurance, water, gas, food, clothing, transportation, etc.

- Discretionary. These include luxury items, vacations, gifts, sports tickets, social outings and eating out, etc.

Once you understand how you're spending your money and where you can make cuts or put spending limits, you can decide what percentage of that income will go into an emergency fund and stock investing. Next, it will be time to set up an emergency fund. This is the money you set aside to pay for unexpected expenses. I would start with a goal of $1000, and then once you hit it, you can expand it. Having a retirement fund is also good, but this one should be a top priority because it will become the foundation for the financial stability you need to achieve complete freedom. Now that this is in progress, it's time to consider mid-term goals. For your mid-term goals, it's time to start thinking about life insurance and disability income insurance. If you're young and have student loans to pay off, focus on that first. This is also where you can consider buying your first or vacation home. A dream car, dream home, or college for your children also falls into this category. When you have your list, determine how much you need to start making and saving to move in that direction.

For your long-term goals, think about the future and how you want life to be. For most people, that vision is retirement with enough money to travel the world, a big home, and enough money in the bank to live a comfortable lifestyle. Visualize your future, allow yourself to dream, and then estimate what that will cost. Do you want to own two houses? Do you want an apartment in the South of France? What is that lifestyle for you, and how much will it cost? A little Google research can help you determine some numbers to help you figure out the expenses. Then with some simple math and assistance from your financial planner, you should know precisely how much money you should save each year to move toward that dream. Once you have a complete (or relatively clear) picture of your financial plan, making an investment plan becomes easy. Why? Because now you understand your objectives, and you know where you stand.

Depending on your current financial situation and goals and how much you are willing to invest, your broker will advise you on the best investments to get started. If you have a small investment budget, you might need to start small, which I always recommend, and things like Penny Stock Investing, ETFs, etc., might be the best way to go. Refrain from assuming; ask for professional advice not from a friend or family member but from a qualified investment or financial advisor.

How To Save More Money Easily

Even as you focus on investing and wealth creation, saving money is essential. The more money you save, the more you'll have to invest, advancing your wealth creation efforts.

Remember what I said earlier? Two main elements needed to build wealth are time and money. Creating more time may not be possible, but you can generate more cash through savings. With those savings, you can reinvest, buy more significant stocks, and diversify your portfolio even more. Here are a few ideas to help you get started.

Pay off credit cards in full each month. That will discipline you to spend only what you know you can afford, and it will shave off those high-interest rates.

Stop impulse or "sales" shopping. You'd be surprised how much money you'll save if you stop buying things because they are on sale or discounted. If you don't need it and it's not making you money - don't buy it.

Brown, bag your lunch to work. If you spend $5 per day for lunch, yet homemade lunch made the night before would only cost you $1.50, then in a year, you'd have saved an extra $840 ($1200 - $360). That's an emergency fund, and you still get some money left over to give yourself a treat.

Stay away from getting rich quick schemes and fads. This is such a money waste for many investors. Please stop giving money to someone who promises a magic bullet or shortcut to get rich. There's no such thing! Stick to tried and true investments and only invest in what you know.

Don't go cheap on your broker and accountant. You'll waste way more money if you choose the wrong broker and financial advisor because they are more affordable. So, save money in the long run by selecting reputable companies and individuals to support, advise, and guide you on this journey. Stop eating out and clubbing every weekend. As long as you spend money on bottles and pay for dinners every weekend to impress people, you'll struggle to grow your wealth. If you don't need to eat out, stay home and cook a healthy meal. Spending money, you don't have to impress people who don't even matter, wastes time and money that you could pour into investment opportunities.

Cancel your subscriptions. It may not seem like much money but add up how much it costs you to have all those streaming apps for sports, movies, entertainment, and other unnecessary software apps that you probably need to remember why you signed up for. You'll soon realize it's a lot. You don't have to cancel everything, but you don't need Netflix, Amazon Prime, Hulu, etc., all at once.

Tips for Making More Money

While saving money and paying off your debt is prudent and wise, learning how to make more money is equally important. We must learn how to make money outside of a regular day job. It's not a class taught in any school (even business school). So, if you're thinking, "I need a way to make more money to fast-track my investment journey," this will help.

Creating a Business

Many individuals have started a start-up or a side hustle and turned it into a giant profit-making machine. Mainly thanks to the Internet, ordinary people like you and me who had nothing have created businesses that turned them into millionaires. You can do the same with little to no money.

Purchasing a Business

Why start something from scratch when you can purchase a turnkey solution and start operating for profit almost immediately? If you know what you're doing and get a good deal, purchasing a business can instantly amplify your net worth and enable you to make huge strides toward your financial freedom. Facebook bought Instagram about a year after its inception. While it seemed like they paid money for it then, it's worth less than the billion Zuckerberg initially paid.

Commodities

Beyond stock investing, you can also build your wealth quickly and more safely, according to most experts, by trading commodities. It's a diversification strategy used by many experienced investors. They use it for long-term investing or to park cash during bearish markets. Entities include precious metals, energy, agricultural produce, and even unique collectibles. Just because most people don't see it as risky and volatile as individual stocks doesn't mean it's risk-free, so make sure you know what you're getting into.

Real Estate and Properties

This is one of the oldest forms of wealth creation. Oprah has often been quoted stating that she loves buying houses like most women love shoes. I don't think she believes them just for fun (although she probably has fun doing it). Real estate investing is less liquid and more cumbersome, but it's one of the least risky ways to make your money work for you. Regardless of the market fluctuations, people will always need a roof over their heads. If you choose the right kind of real estate, that is wealth appreciation that you can bank on.

These are just a few ways to make money and catapult yourself into a future of complete financial freedom and early retirement. Take it one step at a time, invest your time, money, and resources in what you know and resonate with, then expect to reap the rich rewards of your hard work as the years roll on.

Afterword

You made it to the end of this book, and that's a tangible demonstration that you are committed to making this financial dream a reality. In summary, I want to remind you of key concepts as you begin your investment journey. Depending on your personality, risk tolerance, and wealth objectives, you must understand what kind of investor you want to become. Once you know your identity, you can easily play to your strengths and become a more passive or active investor. This will also help you determine your financial goals, investment goals, and what kind of broker to choose.

The next important step is to outline your budget, create an emergency fund, and set some money aside as your capital for investing. Learn about the marketplace (the stock exchanges) and the right ones to research the stocks you'll buy. Take your time with this learning process because the more due diligence you do, the better you'll be once you purchase the stock. If you're going to do penny stock investing, remember that game doesn't happen in the primary markets, and you're better off mastering the process so you can DIY the process and save your profits. If you go for the big players, make sure your fundamental and technical analysis is on point because you'll be throwing money away with these skills and a solid strategy. We've outlined how to pick the right stocks, where to find them, and use metrics such as price-earnings ratio, dividend yield, earnings per share, etc., so implement everything you've learned before making that first purchase.

Investment education and the right mindset will make a difference in this journey. I need help to iterate the importance of continued education and continually working on your relationship with money. Your emotions and psychological state could make or break you in this game.

To become an elite investor and carve out your financial future, you must surround yourself with experts and educational materials to help you become fluent in investments before real exponential growth occurs. That doesn't mean you become a passive consumer and never actually act. Instead, it means you take time to learn as much as possible. Perhaps even Δ you get started the right way and avoid the overwhelm and frustration most newbies usually experience.

Investing and financial freedom processes. Keep learning, experimenting, and acting consistently, and you'll soon be living the life of your dreams.

Thank You

You could have picked from hundreds of other books, but you bought mine, and I appreciate it. Thank you so much for purchasing my book.

Not that you enjoyed (I hope) my book, can I ask you for a tiny favor? Can you please post a review on the platform? You posting a review is the best way to support the work of independent authors like me.

Your feedback will help me keep writing the books that will help you get the desired results. It means a lot to me to hear from you.

I am happy for anyone to reach out to me for help, comments, collaboration ideas, or feedback at

brian@brianscottfitzgerald.com

Visit my author page with this link or Scan this QR code

https://www.amazon.com/author/brianscottfitzgerald.

Additional Resources

Department of Management Sciences, The Islamia University of Bahawalpur, Pakistan. (2013). *https://www.idosi.org/mejsr/mejs-r17(11)13/16.pdf.* Retrieved from https://www.idosi.org/mejsr/mejs- r17(11)13/16.pdf

Stock Market Glossary | Stock Trading Terms Dictionary. (n.d.). Retrieved April 1, 2020, from https://www.firstrade.com/content/en- us/education/glossary

Broker Recommendations Explained. (n.d.). Retrieved April 1, 2020, from https://www.fnarena.com/index.php/broker-recommendations-explained/

Advisers, W. (2017, July 4). Do broker recommendations add value? Retrieved April 1, 2020, from https://www.wrenadvisers.-com.au/2015/07/broker-recommendations/

Reinkensmeyer, B. (2020, March 12). 10 Great Ways to Learn Stock Trading in 2020. Retrieved April 1, 2020, from https://www.stock- trader.com/learn-stock-trading/

Byrnes, T. (2018, March 24). We Asked Our Pros For Tips to Stay Calm During the Market Turmoil. Retrieved April 1, 2020, from https://www.thestreet.com/how-to/how-to-stay-calm-during-market-turmoil-14533003

Samurai, F. (2020, March 9). How To Make Lots Of Money During The Next Downturn. Retrieved April 1, 2020, from https://www.fi- nancialsamurai.com/how-to-make-lots-of-money-during-the-next- downturn/

Frankel, M. C. (2019, May 17). Investing and Taxes: What Beginners Need to Know. Retrieved April 1, 2020, from https://www.fool.- com/the-ascent/buying-stocks/articles/investing-and-taxes-what- beginners-need-to-know/

Stocks. (2019, June 6). Retrieved April 1, 2020, from https://www.in- vestopedia.com/stocks-4427785

How to read a stock chart. (n.d.). Retrieved April 1, 2020, from https://www.moneyunder30.com/how-to-read-a-stock-chart

Snow, R. (2020, January 14). Technical vs. Fundamental Analysis in Forex. Retrieved April 1, 2020, from https://www.dailyfx.com/education/why-trade-forex/technical-vs-fundamental-analysis.html

The Complete Dividend Investing Course (Updated 2020). (n.d.). Retrieved April 1, 2020, from https://www.udemy.com/course/how- to-value-dividend-stocks/

Common Stock. (2020, January 31). Retrieved April 1, 2020, from https://www.investopedia.com/terms/c/commonstock.asp

Brokers, I. (n.d.). Individuals | Interactive Brokers. Retrieved April 1, 2020, from https://www1.interactivebrokers.com/en/home.php

Fidelity. (n.d.). Fidelity Investments - Retirement Plans, Investing, Brokerage, Wealth Management, Financial Planning and Advice, Online Trading. Retrieved April 1, 2020, from https://www.fi-delity.com/

Charles Schwab Trading Stocks. (n.d.). Trading Stocks. Retrieved April 1, 2020, from https://www.schwab.com/stocks

TD Ameritrade Investment Guidance. (n.d.). Investment Guidance & Insights | TD Ameritrade. Retrieved April 1, 2020, from https://www.tdameritrade.com/investment-guidance.page

www.ingramcontent.com/pod-product-compliance
Lightning Source LLC
LaVergne TN
LVHW100319210926
848480LV00003B/1188
* 9 7 9 8 3 4 9 5 3 3 6 8 6 *